United in Service

United in Sacrifice

The members of the Rochester Veterans Writing Group would like to thank Tim Hansen and Mary Finucane for starting the group in August 2014. Had they not done so we would have never met, and this book would never have been written.

United in Service

United in Sacrifice

Written by Veterans and family members of
the Rochester Veterans Writing Group
Rochester, NY

Omega Man Press
Rochester, New York

United in Service, United in Sacrifice
by Rochester Veterans Writing Group

Publication Copyright © 2020
Omega Man Press
Rochester, New York
www.ieWriter.com

All rights reserved. No part of this book may be reproduced or transmitted in any form or by any means, electronic or mechanical, including photocopying, recording, or by any information storage and retrieval system, without the written permission of the publisher, except where permitted by law. ©Rochester Veterans Writing Group 2020.

ISBN: 978-0-9700441-6-7

Edited by GreenShadow Press, Rochester, New York

Contents

WORLD WAR II 1

This Is Living, *Joe Mele* 2

The Steel Coffin, *Kurt Feuerherm* 21

The Apennines and Life and Death, *Kurt Feuerherm* 26

Dienstglas, *Robert (Bob) Whelan* 34

My Wonderful Aunt Jackie, *Robert (Bob) Whelan* 38

Sausages Anyone? *Robert (Bob) Whelan* 61

The Healing Power of Time, *Robert (Bob) Whelan* 66

The Snow Man, *Robert (Bob) Whelan* 70

Just Briggin' Soldiers, *Anonymous* 71

KOREAN WAR AND PRE-VIETNAM 75

Jake—From the Grave, *Charles F. Willard* 76

Ike's Skysweepers, *Vaughn Stelzenmuller* 81

Veterans, Our Grandfathers, *Michael John Lemke* 84

VIETNAM 87

Flying the T-37, *Charles F. Willard* 88

Flying the T-33, *Charles F. Willard* 93

Flying the C-130, *Charles F. Willard* 97

Overheat!, *Charles F. Willard* 107

The Congo Caper, *Charles F. Willard* 111

Air Crash, *Charles F. Willard* 118

"Waterboarding," Air Force Style, *Charles F. Willard* 122

Cheating Death, *Charles F. Willard* 125

Boots in the Air, *Charles F. Willard* 127

Angel of Death or Peace, *Gary T. Redlinski* 128

"Two years were two days, too long" *Gary T. Redlinski* 130

"Der Opfergang" *Vaughn Stelzenmuller* 134

Three Stripes, and I'm In, *Vaughn Stelzenmuller* 136

Accidental Leadership Lessons at the Rifle Range, *Vaughn Stelzenmuller* 138

Textbook Soldier, *Vaughn Stelzenmuller* 141

"Praise the Lord, and Pass the Coffee" *Vaughn Stelzenmuller* 143

A Tale of Two Horribles, *Vaughn Stelzenmuller* 145

A Call for Help, from 1969, *Vaughn Stelzenmuller* 148

Homecoming, *Vaughn Stelzenmuller* 150

1970s AND 1980s 153

A Military Homefront Experience, *Sue Spitulnik* 154

Asking for Help, *Rori Murrell* 172

A Desire to Serve, *Rori Murrell* 174

Day Care, *Joe Mele* 176

IRAQ, AFGHANISTAN, OTHER PLACES 179

War Zones, *Janice Priester-Bradley* 180

How to Heal a Wound, *Janice Priester-Bradley* 181

Costs, *Janice Priester-Bradley* 182

Loss, *Janice Priester-Bradley* 183

Rollover Training, *John Steele* 184

Bin Laden, *John Steele* 193

Terry Jones, *John Steele* 201

BP Cuff, *John Steele* 204

Marine, *Suzanne Dianetti* 206

Wedding Plans, *Suzanne Dianetti* 209

The Incredible Mr. E., *Tim Hansen* 213

Dover, *Tim Hansen* 216

Shovel Dance, *Steve McAlpin* 220

But I Have Promises To Keep, *Mary Finucane* 224

Beneath the Tree of Life, *Michael John Lemke* 227

Out of the Tomb of the Unknown Soldier, *Michael John Lemke* 229

A Fallen Warrior, *Michael John Lemke* 231

Alien-Nation, *Michael John Lemke* 234

FAST FORWARD FLASHBACK, *Michael John Lemke* 236

Death, *Holly Katie* 239

Medal of ExHonorAte, *Holly Katie* 241

Memorial Cards, *Holly Katie* 242

I, Too, *Holly Katie* 243

Over It, *Holly Katie* 245

And the Fruit Rolled Away from the Crabapple Tree, *Holly Katie* 246

Untitled, *Holly Katie* 252

The Big Demon, *Holly Katie* 253

H-E-L+L-P, *Holly Katie* 255

CONTRIBUTORS 257

PROMPTS 269

Tribute to Charles "Mike" Hill

Mike Hill served in the 102 Army Corps of Engineers, and was stationed in Pleiku, Vietnam from 1968-70. He joined RVWG in September 2017, when he moved to Rochester to be near his aging in-laws. We lost him suddenly to a heart attack on January 21, 2019. It was then that we learned his given name was Charles. Mike loved to supply the prompts for our monthly meeting and we all envied his super neat hand-printing with no cross-outs when he wrote in his notebook. He shared his military career with us with no shame and often made us laugh. He once explained the route he traveled on Veterans Day to get the most out of all the free meals and beverages that were offered at area eateries. In his own words, "I have free food down to a science." Unfortunately we were unable to include any of his personal writings but we do have the message left on the Writers and Books answering machine by Mike Warner from the Rochester Genealogical Society upon hearing of his friend's passing. It follows:

> *"I had a very harsh homecoming from Korea in 1972 as so many guys from Vietnam did as well. Those we picked up in Hawaii and landed in CA had a surprise "welcome" waiting. The next two years in South Miami were not any better. The anti-war sentiment was taken out wholesale on active service people and then Veterans as I'm sure you know. The separation and return to Rochester was worse. Returning to college at RIT was a bad anti Veteran experience. My local*

American Legion rejected me. For some 20 years I never even admitted that I was a Vet.

"Mike Hill drew me out. He encouraged me to begin writing about my service experiences. Ft. Dix. in Jersey, Ft. Bliss in TX. A year at a Nike battery in Ohio. Thirteen months in Korea. Two years at the Nike System in Miami. He was right. So. As I began to write and capture what I did, where I was and who I was at that time—my tension relaxed. Damn, I miss the little guy. He helped me heal some 45 years later. He was that good and that kind. Yeah, well, the old dog is getting choked up."

"I will miss him. Dearly. If you want to share this, feel free."

Tribute to Kurt Feuerherm

Kurt Feuerherm was one of our beloved WWII vets. He was born in Germany in 1925 and emigrated to the U.S. when he was six. Years later when serving with the U.S. Army he was often asked to act as an interpreter while stationed in Italy. He is an internationally known abstract artist, but we rarely heard about his fame in the art world. With us he shared his war experiences, his love of bullfrogs, owls, nature in general, and his family. He once told us about being hungry while on active duty so he and a buddy dropped live charges into a lake killing the fish. Without thought of getting in trouble, they took their "catch" to the camp cook to prepare for supper. He said "We all ate well that evening. Everyone was thankful and we didn't get reprimanded." We share a slice of his memoirs in the WWII section of this book.

Kurt and daughter Lisa

"Owls" is a three-dimensional card stock/watercolor/ink art piece done by Kurt Feuerherm in 2016, used with permission of owner Sue Spitulnik

Preface

Mary Finucane and I started RVWG as a means for vets and family members to come together and to write of their military experiences both on the front lines and at home. For some, it was a way to vent, for others, a way to gain stronger writing skills, and still for others, a way to heal the inner wounds of war. Through reading and sharing their stories, the bonds of friendship grew and the community of veterans became a little more connected.

When we held our first workshop in August 2014, only one veteran showed up. After sending out press releases across Rochester, New York, we were delighted that one veteran thought enough of our workshop to attend. The population of veterans in the Rochester area was, and still is around 47,000.

We were struck with the power of this Vietnam vet's command of detail. He was a gunner on a Huey H1-H. He was fired upon and fired back. He wrote of loss and blood running across the floorboards of his gunship. It was some of the most gripping prose we have heard on the Vietnam War. And, he never returned.

"So it goes," as novelist and Army veteran Kurt Vonnegut once wrote.

Slowly but steadily our ranks grew, and we finally found a secure refuge in which to meet and write, thanks to Writers & Books on University Avenue. We owe a debt of gratitude to Joe Flaherty and his staff, who listened to our proposal and allowed us to meet for two to three hours on the first Saturday of each month.

Eventually a core group formed ranging from WW II vets to Korea, Vietnam, the Cold War, Iraq and Afghanistan. All have a story or two to tell.

We feel close to all the members of this group. We have listened to their stories, and they have become our friends. The stories in the following pages ring true with service, sacrifice, heartbreak, and resilience....

    Tim Hansen & Mary Finucane
    Rochester, New York
    January 3, 2020

WORLD WAR II

This Is Living

Joe Mele

World War II

My father's faded Army green backpack was the prize I was allowed to wear in the late 1950's and early 1960's. Although it fell to my knees, I'd sling it over my scrawny shoulders when the neighborhood boys and I ran around the summertime suburban yards, ducking behind trees and fences, scrambling across sun-hot asphalt driveways, finding cover in rows of shrubs, re-enacting the latest episode of *Combat*. As we all refused to play the role of a Nazi, the foe was imaginary. "I'm hit, I'm hit! Medic!" we'd yell after an enemy sniper found his mark. Somehow we survived every time. In our young imaginations the glory of certain victory came quickly and easily.

"War is Hell" my father would say, the few times he talked about WWII. For the most part he wanted to put the war behind him, immersing himself in his medical practice and reveling in suburban family life. Grilling chicken or burgers over charcoal in the backyard, martini in hand, Bermuda shorts showing off his skinny legs, was a favorite fair weather activity. With a big grin, he'd say to me: "Son, this is living." Often playing on the big cabinet stereo in the living room was Dean Martin's "Memories are Made of This."

My father's wartime experience, including 194 continuous days of combat, would sometimes make itself known by an angry outburst or an impassioned rant against a perceived injustice. There was no intentional malice or physical violence.

The threat of "the strap," however, was invoked when all other parental ploys failed. If my or my sister's brattiness became particularly objectionable and uncontrollable, my father took off his belt, doubled it up and snapped it producing a startling crack. There was no need to actually apply belt to behind. We were suitably intimidated. Our behavior was modified, at least temporarily. Now we look back with a smile or a laugh, and a somewhat more understanding perspective on the challenges of raising children.

My mother passed away in 2012. Among her saved things we found hundreds of letters, many of them air mail and V-mail from the WWII years when my father was a surgeon for the 749th Tank Battalion as they fought through France, Belgium, and Germany. The content moving and poignant; as I read, I felt I was intruding on their lives. I kept reading. With each letter, in my mind, an old movie projector started up; the whir of the motor, the heat from the light bulb, the slow spinning of the big reel, the black and white moving images on the portable screen in a room half darkened by closed venetian blinds. And the past came to me in a series of mini one-act plays, looking like something Frank Capra directed.

Today, at 67 years old, I'm putting on that faded army green backpack again, and envisioning the WWII experience through my father's then 30-year-old eyes.

***

After a long courtship, Joseph and Antoinette (my father and mother-to-be) married on April 26, 1941. Joseph had graduated from the University of Buffalo Medical School and completed his internship at St. Mary's hospital in Rochester, NY. His father could not have been prouder, having scrimped and saved on an electrician helper's salary to put Joseph through college and medical school during Great Depression years. Antoinette had graduated from the Highland Hospital Nursing School, earning the admiration of her family as well as her RN. Together, they were working to attract a critical mass of patients to his fledgling private general practice. The office was attached to the first floor of their newly purchased two-story home on Jay Street in Rochester, NY. The second floor was rented out. The house was on a busy corner, with a hair salon next door, a grocery store across the street, and a funeral home on the other corner. Buses stopped just outside the front door, leaving a cloud of fumes as they rumbled on. Once the practice was up and running, they hoped to start a family. The promise of America was slowly becoming fulfilled for these first generation Italian-Americans.

***

Since the Lend/Lease Act of March 11, 1941, the United States had been officially supporting England and the other allied nations in their fight against the Axis Powers. It wasn't until December 8, 1941, the day after Japanese bombers, fighters and torpedo planes attacked Pearl Harbor, that the United States declared war on Japan. Three days later, Germany and Italy declared war on the US, and the country was all in.

The US Army had been ramping up its numbers from 189,389 in 1939 to 1,647,477 by December 1941. In 1940 Congress had passed the first peacetime draft, requiring men between the ages of twenty-one and thirty-six to register. Despite the increase, the army was poorly prepared when the Declaration of War was made. The army could muster 17 defensive divisions ready for combat. For offensive action, there were one infantry division, two artillery brigades and five antiaircraft regiments ready. Germany was conquering the world with 180 divisions.

To achieve an army large enough to take on the axis powers, a wide net was cast. Though the physical standards were low, many recruits failed even these minimal requirements because of health reasons. Many of the health problems were attributed to poor nutrition during the Great Depression. In the fall of 1942, Congress passed a bill expanding the age range for draftees to eighteen to thirty-seven.

At 30 years old, with his small but growing medical practice, Joseph thought and hoped the call to serve would not come his way, at least for a while depending on the progress of the war, but the Army needed doctors. "I have patients who depend on me. Civilians need doctors too," he argued. The Army needed doctors, and it was put to him this way: "You can volunteer as a lieutenant, or we can draft you as a corporal." And so Lieutenant Joseph Mele put aside his dreams and aspirations, and began his US army career. On Nov. 23, 1942, Joseph and Antoinette left by car from cold and snowy Rochester, NY, and arrived at the somewhat warmer Camp Barkeley, TX, on Nov. 28.

In their case, the quarters for a married officer was a small drafty bungalow in Brownsville, TX. Cold in the winter and hot in the summer was the order of the day. That bug skittering across the floor was likely to be a scorpion. Dark places were their favorite haunt, so it became habit to shake out shoes or boots before sticking a foot into one.

Joe's time was monopolized in the daytime at the Medical Replacement Training Center and at night reading the 1007-page <u>Military Medical Manual.</u> Toni (Antoinette) found some friends among the other officers' wives.

At the much-needed break provided by the December 25th Christmas Dinner in the Officer's Mess at Camp Barkeley, they were accompanied by Ed and Ruth Malachowaski from Chicago, IL. The food was quite good, and there was a lot of it.

The menu is below:

Officers' Mess
Medical Replacement Training Center

Christmas 1942
Camp Barkeley, Texas

United in Service ★ United in Sacrifice

Christmas Menu
December 25, 1942

Relish Tray
Stuffed Eggs Russee   Hearts of Lettuce   Sardine Canapes
Fresh Shrimp   Stuffed Olives   Sweet Relish
Fruit Cup, Grenadine
Consomme Entasse, Princess
Individual Mold Vegetable Salad
Fried Milk-Fed Chicken, Southern Style
Giblet and Mushroom Gravy
Parslied Boiled New Potatoes
Marshmallow Sweet Potatoes
Buttered White Asparagus Tips
Buttered Fresh Green Peas
Individual White Cake   Fruit Cake
Pumpkin Pie
Coffee   Tea
Candy   Cigars   Nuts

Guests of Members $1.00

World War II

In time, the training moved from the classroom into the field. This piece from the March 28, 1943 edition of TANK TALK, published bi-weekly by the enlisted men of the 747th Tank Battalion, Camp Hood, TX, provides some humorous insight. It's titled "MEDICAL DETACHMENT OPERATES WITH SKILL and DISPATCH":

> Lt. Mele's 'pillrollers' were complimented freely on the excellent manner in which they performed their duties on the recent laceration marathon carried out on the fatal number three Commando Course.
>
> Maj. Sleator, inspector instructor of the course, remarked that our medics were the best posted crew he had seen to date.
>
> Exact statistics are lacking, but 1st Sgt. Filinuk says that somewhere in the neighborhood of 11 barrels of iodine were used, (some neighborhood). At any rate ALL the adhesive tape was expended (more was sent for), much of it however, in the name of modesty; the barbed wire barricade making exposed posteriors the order of the day.
>
> A thousand and some cuts, scratches and bruises were treated. One operation performed on the field, saw Pvt. Melluso take six stitches in a torn fingere [sic]; he certainly can take it. Didn't even grimace.
>
> More vital statistics were these: eight cases of measles (7 in A Co.) Pvt. Anthony Ferraro (A Co.) fracture of the left knee, off the 15 foot wall. Pvt. Albert Bernand (Hq. Co.) hip injury off the 15 foot wall. P.F.C Eddie Ling (C Co.) fractured ankle sustained in Close Combat fighting. Sgt. F. Southern, broken figure [sic], also on Judo stuff.

```
Those men weren't as lucky as Joe Rapp of
Service Co., who fell off the rope platform
(25 feet high) lit on his back (he's a 260
pounder) and didn't even chip a fingernail.
```

My Father told me a story that could have occurred during this same training exercise. It was his responsibility to provide first aid to the participating soldiers. He set up medic stations at key points along the route. One aspect of the training was a five-mile slog. He was slim, but hadn't yet developed the endurance demanded of a long run—his work requiring and his inclination leaning toward more intellectual pursuits. As he was panting, sweating and trudging along the dusty Texas road, he flagged down a passing truck and hitched a ride. "Everybody runs," said the Captain who spotted him. "Sir, I can run, or I can oversee the First Aid Stations—can't do both" replied Lt. Mele with all the sincere conviction he could muster. The Captain's face showed he wasn't buying it, but he did not press the issue, and for another day, Lt. Mele was saved from physical fitness.

His training took him in succession to these camps:

- Camp Barkeley, TX (NOV 1942 -> FEB 1943)
- Camp Hood, TX (MAR 1943 -> JUN 1943)
- Camp Bowie, TX (JUL, 1943 -> SEP 1943)
    - promoted to Captain on September 13, 1943
    - reassigned from the 747th to the 749th Tank Battalion
- Camp Polk, LA (OCT 1943 -> DEC, 1943)
- Camp Swift, TX (DEC, 1943-> FEB 1944)

It wasn't all work and no play. On Monday MAR 8, 1943, Toni, who was still living in the bungalow in Brownsville, wrote this letter to Joe at Camp Hood:

> My Darling Husband,
>
>   The postman just delivered two letters from you, one from Joe D, one from Lil, and another from the Milners. Of course, I saved yours until the last so that I could enjoy them thoroughly. They were beautiful letters, and I think you are anxious to learn my views on a certain subject.
>
> It all began when I was about 7 days late and I thought that I would start sending you Jr's love also, but when I found out it was not true, like you - I was sorry and glad - Sorry because I knew (even before you had said so in your letter) that you would want me to go home and be taken care of, and I did not like the idea of being away from you. Glad - because I know you would love to be called Daddy - and if the day ever came when you would be sent to a place where I could not be with you (I don't like to think or talk of that), but We both know that there is such a possibility - Well, then I would have someone that would be a part of you. I don't think that I would be afraid of the idea because there have been worse cases than mine on record, and as long

as I were in capable hands, I wouldn't worry - I don't think. There is another angle - I simply know that you would want to grow with the heir (or heiress) because it would be such a new experience that you would enjoy the thrills of fatherhood; but if you had to go away, then he would miss your influence, and I am sure that yours is the good influence - That is a complicated sentence but I am sure that you can unravel it. Have I made myself clear, darling?

Joe D. Wrote that he has received the cigarettes we sent and that he will send us a picture just as soon as he has one taken. He expects to get a leave in April before reporting to Ellis Island - What do they do there? This week he is studying carburetion and lubrication. Lily writes that Barr will leave March 17 and will she be lonesome. The law firm of Scully and Obrien sent you a check for $32.00, and Pappy will deposit it in the bank. She also says that she has gained some weight. The film that Helen sent also arrived today.

I think I have read your letter a dozen times already this morning and they were delivered about an hour ago. I shall read them over again to see if there are any other questions to answer.

You do have a problem with that neurotic patient. Don't you think that psychiatric treatments would help, or is he too unintelligent for that sort of thing?

By the way, Lil saw "Random Harvest," and she thinks it is a truly wonderful picture and that we would enjoy it - So we shall simply have to see it.

It is warmer out today, and you know how glad I am about that.

Well, my darling, I think I shall write to Lil next. So keep warm and I shall pray for Capt. Dwyer's prompt return.

  All my love and kisses,

  Toni

P.S. - I am now going out to sweep the car. Since I have to pick up a few girls tomorrow, I might just as well clean the inside anyway.

  Love,

  Toni

Mrs. Donaldson said that it seems to her we are always using our car. She is nice.

  Love,

  Toni

Here is Joe's reply of MAR 11, 1943:

Dearest Toni,

Now you know the sad news dear. You don't know how hard it was for me to sit down yesterday + write you the sad news. I know just how this is going to affect you, but it hurts me just as much too. Here I am back from a day in the field. I didn't do much at all but I feel tired. I wouldn't have minded it at all if I were going home in 3-4 days but now every day drags on and I am just existing. I am not going to count the days anymore. The more I keep track of how soon I will be home the longer the time grows. So I am going to keep on hoping but there are no definite plans in my mind. Liar that I am, already I am thinking of a week from this Saturday or Sunday when we come back from the field hoping that Captain Dwyer will be back.

It seems that now when we both had decided that it was perfectly all right to go thru with a certain plan that we have been postponing for almost 2 years, fate keeps us apart. Yes dear, you were right when you said I would love to be called Daddy by an heir and by my darling wife. I know that you love children + you have found out that I do also. I keep thinking how happy we would be at home preparing for an event like that + how happy we would be with the *child. We would probably spoil the little brat like I tell everyone else not to do but we would be so happy. Then I compare that with the life that we are leading + well, I just keep wishing that the war hadn't come + we could have our dream. It is almost 2 years + we have been perfectly + I mean perfectly happy. I have never regretted our marriage for 1 instant. The only thing I regret is that we couldn't have been married sooner so we would have had that much more happiness together. This is quite a talkative + dreamy letter dear but this is how I feel right now. I want to put down + convey to you all these things that I often think of even when we are together, but can't just express in words. Often when we are together reading or listening to the radio I felt so happy just being close to you + knowing that my own beloved + beautiful Toni is next to me, that it isn't necessary for me to speak. I just sit there and glow with happiness + satisfaction. We are really the world's happiest lovers. I have never run into anyone who has been as happy as we + for so long. Maybe some people are as happy as we are on their honeymoon but when that wears off, they go on to being an average couple with constant quarrels. It is because we are so happy that I* miss you so much + wish that we could go back to our normal way of life. I think a good percentage of these fellows who enjoy army life are those who are unhappy at home + so they seek a change. They want a life of adventure + excitement to fill the gap in their life. There is no gap in my life. It is full of happiness + joy + I wish we could go back to it very soon.

Well dear this is a long letter for me to be writing with all the interruptions I have had. The fellows keep wandering in + sit around to shoot the bull. However I finally managed to get most of my thoughts on paper. I always have been this happy with you but this is the first time I have been able to get it down on paper or even say it. So dearest one, keep your chin up + daddy will be home soon + then maybe someday soon I can say momma to my one + only + mean it.

Love to my dearest of all + regrets that we will have to be separated for a little over another week.

    Your loving husband,

    Joe

> *P.S. Keep writing daily even though you may not get regular mail while I am gone on the field.*
>
> *More love,*
>
> *Joe*

The letters continued almost daily and were supplemented with care packages after Joe was deployed to the European Theater of War. The censorship policy in force at the time prevented Joe from going into the details of the Tank Battalion's activity. For the most part, his letters expressed how much he missed Toni, and after December 24, 1943, how much he missed his daughter Joanne. He was not present at her birth. He wouldn't see her in person until she was almost two years old. The letters and photos from Toni kept up Joe's dismal morale in the darkest days of the carnage.

Here's a letter from Joe on Joanne's first birthday:

> *24 December 1944*
> *Somewhere in France*
>
> *My dearest darling Toni + Joanne,*
>
> *First of all Happy Birthday to you Joanne. I am sorry I can't be home to greet you on your 1st birthday. You may think that your Daddy doesn't think very much of you since he wasn't home when you were born + I am not home today. Believe me darling my absence is not voluntary. It is Uncle Sam who prevents me from coming home to you. Again let me wish you the best of luck + many happy returns of the day + I hope +*

pray that I will be home to help you celebrate your second birthday.

By the way before I forget it is Lt. Col Fann now. There may have been other questions that you asked me but I don't remember them just now.

This morning I went to Mass + again feel like a Christian. While I was in Church I was reminded of home. The Church had been hit + the sun was streaming in. A man had a little boy in the seat ahead of me + he kept brushing his hair back. Then a little girl about 6-7 years old passed around the collection plate. There weren't too many G.I.'s around + the church was full of civilians. The whole scene made me very homesick + tears almost came to my eyes.

Gosh darling how I wish you + I were together. The radio is on + I am listening to some orchestra. They have a beautiful harmony effect. I had so much that I was going to write to you but I just can't get my thoughts together. How I curse Hitler + his gang when I realize he is the reason that I missed shopping for Joanne's birthday + Christmas gifts + that I missed being with you and Joanne for so long. It seems like centuries. I am so sick + tired of this life. I want to go back to my family.

I haven't had a bath in about a month. Today I will see if I can heat enough water to take a sponge bath. This life is just an

> existence not living. I just go from day to
> day doing what I must but there is no
> interest here. The only things I care about
> are you + Joanne + I can't have you now.
>   Well darling let me kiss you Good
> Morning with all the Trimmings + try to get
> this letter off this morning. Tomorrow's
> letter will probably sound more depressing
> than this one.
>   All my love + plenty of kisses w/
>   all the trimmings
>   Joe
>   P.S. Please send me another package with
> the usual contents.
>   More love + more trimmings
>   Joe

And so, it's not a war story that these letters hold, but a love story in a time of war. It was a love that lasted a lifetime. Joe's final letter was in an envelope marked "To be read upon my death." Joe died on July 19, 1982. Toni read this a few days later:

> My dearest Toni,
>
> Let me tell you again how deeply I love you. Our years together have been the happiest of my life. Now we are apart.
>
> There will be trying days ahead. Please remember all the happiness we had together + forget whatever problems we had.

Be guided in financial affairs by our good friend Charlie.

Don't be hasty in any decisions.

Be wary of the many demands that will come to you.

Remember to think of yourself more.

Our children each + every one will be of great help in these times.

Thank you darling for a wonderful love. I guess our marriage was made in heaven.

    All my love,

    Joe

The Steel Coffin

Kurt Feuerherm

It was just a huge square hole or hold as they called it in maritime terms.

The place was on a Liberty ship, which I had boarded in Newport News, VA, just south of Washington, DC, around January 1944. My basic training was completed and I had gone back to Buffalo for my two-week leave before being assigned to overseas duty. An extra two weeks had been tacked on to this time because I had become ill with pneumonia. I recovered fast and was reassigned to Fort Meade, MD. Within a week I was walking up the gangplank with 80lbs. of equipment ... knowing that I was going somewhere in the European Theatre of Operations (ETO). Feelings of dread, unknown expectations, loneliness and fear were in my heart as I stepped aboard this gray monster.

An officer came up to me, asked my name, looked on the roster list and found my assignment. It was in B-bunk in row ten in the aft hold. The first thing that struck me was how overcrowded everything was. My bunk was in the middle of a tier of five bunks about ten feet high and not more than two feet between each one. Each canvas bed had grommets attached to a clothesline rope woven around a pipe frame. Each bunk could be folded back when not in use. This gave us more room between the aisles. The hold held about 200 GIs in the most primitive conditions imaginable. Everyone had a sort of vacant stare of unbelieving reality that this was going to be our home for the next three weeks. The constant din, cigarette smoke and odors were at times nauseating. Our only salvation was the deck of the ship.

The first couple days were relatively calm because we were in the inland waterway cruising south to a rendezvous with other ships off the coast of Florida. Our convoy was to be about 120 ships made up of about ten Liberty ships like the one we were on for troop transportation, various freighters, oil tankers, landing craft transports and naval escorts. There was one heavy cruiser, a total of 15 destroyers and destroyer escorts. Off the coast of south Florida the convoy headed due east and zigzagged its way across the Atlantic. About the second day, the weather took a turn for the worse. The seas began to roll and I puked my guts out for two days. In fact, it was amazing that we didn't lose anyone overboard as there were so many of us at the railings. The one saving grace was that it was dry, and the sun was shining even though the ship was pitching. You can imagine what it was like in the hold even though we had slop buckets. Unless you were on the top bunk you were not spared the puke and odors.

I was becoming much more aware of the danger and pitfalls of the Steel Coffin, the name which was given to the hold. In the back of my mind, the images of being caught below deck after being torpedoed were terrifying.

Actually, the rest of the crossing was uneventful, and for about a week we were lulled into complacency by a kind of pleasant existence. It was during this time I became a good friend of another GI named Stu Landon. Stu was pardoned from prison in Kentucky because he volunteered to join the army. He had been imprisoned for gambling and taught me various poker games. We played in the nickel and dime games

World War II

with quite a bit of success. He suggested that we get into the higher stakes game but we needed more cash. Between us we had about $30, which was a lot in those days. Each of us put up $20 for the kitty or bank and we started a keno game, which Stu knew would make us money because we ran the bank. The game was a no-lose situation for us. After we made about $100 we split the money and got into the high-stake poker games. He tutored me and said that after I reached $3,000, I should quit and send the money home to my parents to buy them a home. Well, I won $4,000 and Stu said, "Quit, you've made enough." I said I needed to make a little more and he just shook his head in disappointment. He was right, in two hands I lost it all. Nothing was left and after that I knew gambling was not for me even though it was very tempting. Stu taught me bridge and the rest of the time on the ship that was what I played.

After losing all that money, my days were spent in doing organized calisthenics, playing cards, writing letters and just plain soaking up the sun. The ocean was calm, dotted with all the different kinds of ships. The small landing crafts called LSTs were remarkable in the fact that they were so small and still able to cross the ocean. You could watch the destroyers belching their heavy smoke as they were running their zigzag path trying to find U-boats. The rumors of our destination continued to fly and all of us speculated where we would end up—North Africa, Italy or England. After a little more than two weeks, about half the convoy split off and continued on a northerly direction. I knew then I wasn't going to England. Our part of the convoy made a 90-degree turn toward the east, which took us to the straits of Gibraltar. Later that day, looming up on the left side of the boat we could see the huge rock. I didn't know it at the time, but as we steamed through the straits, a pack of U-boats was accompanying us suspended in the cold current underneath the outgoing warm current of the Mediterranean Sea. Later on, after the war, this fact was discovered, which was the basis of the German movie, *Das Boot*.

    I remember a beautiful sunset that night before going down in the hold which now had become a foul-smelling Dantesque hellhole. Visually, it reminds me now of the Piranesi prints of his fantasy prisons. A few hours after dark I was shaken awake by one of my friends, "Kurt, I think we're being attacked." You could hear the popping and thumping noises drifting down the stairway. We looked at each other with fear and said, "We better get our asses out of here." I jumped out of my bunk and it seemed everyone else was jumping too! There was shouting, swearing, shoving, and pushing—pandemonium resulted! Then the lights went out and all the trapped images came to mind. Luckily, I had plotted an escape route in my mind. I sidled along the outer wall of the hold until I came to the back of the stairway. The officers were trying to keep us calm but at the same time keep us in the hold. It didn't work. Somehow I got past the officers and up the stairs I went. The blast of sea air filled my lungs and told me that I was near the top. Bursting out of the tomb, someone grabbed me and told me to lie flat on the deck. Everyone got out of the hold. Around us a bizarre scene unfolded. First of all, all the ship's anti-aircraft guns were blazing away because the attack was a combined U-boat and Luftwaffe effort. Several tankers were torpedoed and destroyed by unbelievable explosions. The sky was illuminated by tracer bullets that revealed everybody on the deck in an eerie light. I can't tell you what the losses were.

In our vicinity at least 3 ships were lost. The whole attack seemed like it lasted for a couple of hours, but in reality was more like a half hour. For the rest of the night I lay on the deck shivering and shaking ... fear finally leaving me at dawn. I felt lucky that we all escaped the Steel Coffin.

The Apennines and Life and Death

Kurt Feuerherm

It was August of 1944 and the Germans were on the north side of the Arno River. We were on the south side, and about a quarter of a mile on each side of the river was a no-man's land. It was a relatively quiet time consisting mostly of reconnaissance sorties and periodic shellfire. Florence was in shambles. All bridges were down and only the center part of the Ponte Vecchio was standing. The railroad yard was non-functioning from allied bombing and many an historical building had major damage. It was an eerie sight to see such a beautiful city in such shambles. I remember looking at the Santa Trinita Bridge watching people crossing over on the remains, putting their lives in jeopardy on a beautiful sunshiny day. At the time I knew nothing of the historical and artistic value of this marvelous city, a city I grew to love and teach in fifty years later. In late September of 1944, the Allies started an offensive to try to break through the German lines, and enter the Po valley and pressure the Germans from the south to hasten the end of the war in Europe. These final six months were pure hell in my combat life, which ended in June of 1945. How I ever survived that time I have no idea.

The Germans set up a defense line north of Rome along the backbone of the Northern Apennine Mountains. We were really not prepared for this battle. We were without sufficient reserves and the fighting drew to a stalemate as the second winter in Italy set in. Both the American 5th and British 8th armies were drained of men and supplies as units were pulled out for the invasion of Normandy and Southern France. The offensive on the Gothic Line in the north Apennine Mountains began on the 10th of September, a beautiful day. Now we began a push to try and capture the main route from Florence to Bologna. The terrain was steep and desolate, and each ridge had to be occupied. The 85th Division had been in reserve, but the fighting had begun as soon as we crossed the Arno River. I remember crossing just west of the Ponte Vecchio on the makeshift bridge, which had been the Ponte Santa Trinita. After crossing, we advanced along the Via Lungarno to the corridor of the Uffizi Gallery, which was heavily sandbagged. The bullets were flying and ricocheting off the walls of the corridor. It lasted only a short time with the Germans retreating rapidly. The fighting was intense but sporadic along Highway 65, the main route to Bologna. We took the town of Vaglia without much opposition, but the next five miles of the route to San Lorenzo took three days to capture. Our objective was the hill town of Firenzola and the hills around the Futa Pass, a most important cut in the Apennines.

This was to be the hardest, scariest and most intense time for me in combat. By now everybody knew that I could speak fluent German, and I was called upon numerous times to try to persuade and convince the German soldiers to give up. But I was not the only one; there was a staff sergeant, Ludwig, and another private who could speak German. However, for some unknown reason, it seemed that I was the one that usually got the assignment to speak to the Germans. The fighting was intense on a hill just South of Firenzola. My platoon had taken the hill with heavy casualties. We were on the crest of the hill when the Germans counterattacked, and we were beaten back. We regrouped and now it was our turn to counterattack. I wasn't sure what was happening when all of a sudden, three German soldiers jumped out of bushes and immediately held up their hands and surrendered. I wasn't sure of their actions or intentions, so I shouted in German for them to lie flat on the ground and left them there to be picked up by someone in the rear. The situation was very tense, and Sergeant Ludwig told them in German that they should stay prone, and nothing would happen to them. I overhead one of the Germans say to the other, "Christ, they all speak German!" We couldn't help but laugh. In another ten minutes we had six more prisoners who were glad the war was over for them. Our counterattack was successful and Firenzola was ours.

What struck me about this part of my combat experience was how easy it was to overrun the enemy in the dense mountain terrain north of Florence. It was bitter cold, numbing and miserable. The temperature in the fall and winter was always below freezing. There was a thick fog that you could get lost in. The fighting in the Apennines was exhausting to the point that we couldn't go on, and ended up spending the winter in a stalemate. Of the numerous firefights that I was in, one in particular stands out. It happened in late October somewhere near the Futa Pass. Our intelligence had pinpointed a heavily forested hill that was strategic and had to be occupied. A small unit of Germans was in control of the area. We were given orders by headquarters to take control of the hill in a predawn attack. I will never forget it. In my life, it was the high point of fear and danger.

There had been a light snow in the night. The weather had cleared and the moon was almost full. We were tired but alert, and as slowly and quietly as possible moved along a moonlit pathway to our objective. We were not sure where the Germans were. Our lieutenant said he wanted me by his side in case the Germans decided to surrender....Ha!....Ha! Well, what happened was we completely overran the position, and before we knew it, we were in the midst of sleeping Germans. Then, all hell broke loose. Total chaos. No one knew who anyone was, and as soon as one shot was fired, everyone began shooting. I dove into the foxhole that one of the Germans had dug and landed on top of another GI named Alex. There we lay on top of each other, about eight feet away from a German, who was machine-gunning at random. His shots flew over my head and shredded a fallen log, so that I was covered with wood chips. What was going through my mind was that this was it. *I am dead meat!* Alex, who was under me, was also convinced that we weren't going to get out of this one. So he handed me a grenade, I pulled the pin and threw it in the direction of the machine gunner. It hit a tree, returned and bounced off my ass and exploded about ten feet down from the foxhole. Luckily, it landed below us when it exploded. I turned over in the foxhole and pitched the next grenade he handed me between two trees, assuming that it was enough to either kill or convince the German to give up. The firefight lasted another five minutes, and all of a sudden ended as quickly as it started. We had prevailed. It always seems so strange to me how quickly a skirmish, firefight, battle or whatever you want to call it was over. Fifteen or twenty minutes is an eternity when your life is on the line. Ten minutes later, the sun rose, and the hill became a scene of death and horror in a beautiful setting—quite surreal.

I recall being among bodies, German prisoners, and the very exhausted men who had stared death in the face. We had won the hilltop at a high cost. Of the twelve men in my squad, three were dead and four were wounded, leaving five of us staring into space. How long can this madness go on?

There were several more intense encounters like the Pine Top knoll firefight and many small skirmishes with the Germans. One in particular that I remember quite vividly was a night encounter that involved my skill as an interpreter. It was a pitch-black night and our platoon leader was convinced that we had surrounded a bunch of German soldiers and wanted to give them the option to surrender. As usual, I was called upon to use my fluency in German. I was told by our lieutenant to tell them that they were surrounded and to lay down their arms and surrender. I cupped my hands over my mouth and shouted the message out into the dark night. The night was bitter cold, and as the moon rose, you could see the vapors rising from our heavy breathing. There was complete silence, and what was about a minute seemed like an eternity. Finally there was a break in the silence, a small chuckle and a voice of the German officer saying, "I don't think so; you are the ones that are surrounded." I turned to the lieutenant and said "Shit, we are in for another one." I don't remember who started firing first. But again, we were in total chaos not knowing who was who. With such fear comes the survival urge, and in this case, everyone was shooting and running for cover. Then everything died down.

I was exhausted, alone behind a tree, and just wondering where I was. No one knew what happened. The dawn light was giving the landscape more definition. A thick fog had made everything look eerie. There was a path next to the tree, and I needed to find out where our platoon was and what happened. The path led to the edge of a field. As I approached the open field about one hundred feet down the path stood a figure, and I shouted, "Company L?"

The figure turned toward me, and by the outline of his helmet, I realized it was a German soldier holding a machine pistol. We stood in silence looking at each other's silhouette. All at once both of us turned and ran like hell. We both had had enough of this insanity. I ran hard toward a haystack in the distance in a wheat field. They looked just like the ones in Monet's paintings. I got to the other side of the haystack, stopped, lay down exhausted, and fell asleep. I woke up an hour later from the sun's heat. I looked around and there was no one in sight; I just didn't know what to do. I then decided that I needed sleep and a break from this goddamn war. I took off my helmet and uniform; I was naked since I didn't have any underwear. I covered all my equipment with loose hay so that no one would know I was there. Stark naked I crawled into the haystack where no one could see me; I fell sound asleep. I slept through the whole day and night and woke up the next morning.

Slowly, as I came out of my heavenly respite, reality came back to me. I heard voices and listened very carefully so I could recognize the language. Was it Italian, German or English? Then I heard a familiar voice in the conversation, and I realized it was my squad leader. I slowly emerged from the haystack and there stood my buddies. I was stark naked, and we all laughed our asses off. Chet told me I had been missing in action for two days and presumed dead. "Get your goddamn clothes on you Heinie bastard and we'll get back to the squad!" The Germans had disappeared and we headed back to the platoon. My little sleep in the haystack was necessary for my survival, but it also made me long for my return to civilian life. I never knew how warm and cozy a haystack could be.

***

The advance into the Po valley had stopped high in the cold and freezing Apennines in early November. Our permanent position became known as the Gothic line. We dug trenches, made dugouts and started to nest. At first our dugouts, or pillboxes, were very rudimentary. The longer we were there, the more elaborate this temporary home became. For example, the roofs at first were hardly any protection against incoming artillery with only a few inches of dirt cover. By the time of the March Spring offensive there would be three feet of dirt covering our heads. We also installed 50-gallon drum stoves and were very cozy. The walls were lined with mud and straw for insulation. Our duties at the time were quite monotonous; mostly scouting missions, observation, and 96wire-laying assignments.

Our defensive line was on a high ridge in the Apennines near the Futa Pass. It consisted of trenches, our dugouts, and listening posts, which were farther down the ridge and very open to enemy fire. We had very little movement during the daytime. Almost everything was done under the cover of dark night. Moonlight was eerie and stationary images came alive. On one such night three of us, myself, Stanley and Sgt. Baker (our squad leader) were sent by headquarters out to repair some communication lines, which were destroyed during the usual morning artillery bombardment from the Germans. The moonlight was bright, so we had pretty good vision for our mission. We had to cross a ravine to lay some new wire. I had the canister of wire and was leading the way. It had snowed late that evening and everything was covered with about an inch of snow.

At the bottom of the ravine we came across five dead German soldiers. I stepped very carefully over the frozen bodies; several of which were lying on their backs in rigor-mortis poses. It was a strange sight. I struggled to get up the other side of the ravine. When I reached the listening post, I realized I had used up most of the wire. Stanley and the Sergeant were still in the ravine. I pulled on the line to take up the slack; all at once I heard a lot of cursing and shouting: "Holy shit," yelled Stanley, "they're still alive." They scrambled up to the post and were as white as a sheet asserting that two of the Germans had moved and were still alive. We were dumbfounded and finally realized that the wire had caught their arms, causing the body to move from my tightening of the lines. It had scared the shit out of them. Strange things happen in the moonlight, and imaginations can run wild.

Our routine was boring until the spring of 1945 when we left our positions to prepare for the push into the Po Valley. In late April we headed off to the last offensive of the war.

Dienstglas

Robert (Bob) Whelan

This is a pair of WWII German Afrika Korps artillery spotter binoculars. They were labelled "Dienstglas." They were powerful and well-made field glasses with a magnification power of 10. In German "dienst" means service. You could call these "service glasses."

On one occasion in April 1945, I and another soldier had entered a German artillery spotter's location, and had taken its occupants prisoners. After the capture, I had returned to the location and retrieved a pair of these Dienstglases and carried them with me through the remainder of my combat duty time.

My Veteran friend Steve McAlpin and I revisited my European battle sites in July of 2017. Revisiting these sites was a revelation. The views were different than those of our previous experiences. In fact, they were so different that I was inspired to use this Dienstglas as a metaphoric vehicle for my stories of war experience.

My stories are not so much about the details of what happened then, as they are of how we view things and happenings over time. The time component, in my view, is crucial to the understanding of life. Especially those of war and war experience trauma. Time heals when it is combined with forgiveness. My Dienstglas inspired my way of relating it.

Relationships are more about what my stories attempt to describe, than descriptions of conditions and events at one discrete time. Time is the variable in these stories, as well as place.

Below is a picture of me in May 1945, taken when I had an opportunity to check out the remnants of Hermann Goering's elaborate villa at Berchtesgaden, Bavaria.

The Dienstglas is draped around my neck in that picture. I wore them everywhere. I was able to view the last remaining days of WWII through those special and powerful glasses. They gave me two additional sets of lenses from which to view. They were with me right up until about ten years ago, when they mysteriously disappeared.

Their two views are metaphors for duty and respect. Duty in the form of sacrifice and obedience. Respect in the form of acceptance and brotherhood. It is a reference to viewing life through different lenses. Specifically, close up views and at the other end of the binoculars a distant, all encompassing, view. Both are helpful to view life as a balance between *goods* and *bads*. This is the basis of the metaphors I prefer to frequently engage in as I write my stories. Two perspectives, two relationships. Up close, exact narrow view. Far away, a different perspective. A Duality, if you will....

In our return to Germany's Ruhr Valley, Steve and I were able to return to a place where my WWII Dienstglas acquisition happened. Several new variables then entered into our long viewing range. A new perspective was achieved. There was a lot more to be seen in 2017, than there was in 1945.

First, the huge valley where some 300,000 German troops surrendered had been transformed from a dismal gray to an active green. Peace had returned. Prosperity was evident. People were welcoming instead of frightened and hostile. I could not find the artillery spotter house, but assumed it, too, if still existing would not be being used for its wartime purpose. Altogether a more promising view than that of 1945.

Peaceful surroundings result from peaceful actions. A peaceful place is a result of forgiveness. Forgiveness is a major step to brotherhood.

Forgiveness works in many ways. One way is restoration. A restoration of a broken relationship to one of reconciliation. We have spent the last 72 years restoring relationships with our German brethren. We have helped them tear down walls. We have fed them. They have become better in so many ways, as have we, as a result. It would behoove each of us to keep this process alive and growing. Steve and I discussed this as we were observing the good changes we set out to find in our revisiting the past.

The target of these stories is to bracket in on an acceptable target of peace—forgiveness. Without coming close to forgiveness, we are completely missing the target of achieving peace. The enemy of peace is anger.

Putting anger out of harm's way is our mission in life. We are not angry with our German brothers anymore, nor are they with us. We have forgiven each other and are better for it.

Many of the stories I write deal with forgiveness in some way or another. I had a wonderful aunt who forgave me time after time, for all the ways I would anger most people, including my own parents. I was not a model person—far from it, but she saw things in me from a distance that my parents understatedly could not.

What follows are stories of forgiveness. Not so much of combat experiences, but of lessons learned. And, the challenge in them in how they happened over time.

My Wonderful Aunt Jackie

Robert (Bob) Whelan

I begin this series of stories with a reference to my wonderful Aunt Jackie. She is one of those whom I mentioned as distant family members. They serve, too, just like all who are a part of the human family whom we as military Veterans serve. Aunt Jackie was unique, she lived in three centuries. Born in 1900, last year of the 19th Century, died in 2001, first year of the 21st Century. An amazing feat that not many can duplicate. She did a lot of service and she left a lot of service legacy.

Her legacy to me was an addendum to my name: "He meant well."

To me it expressed forgiveness. In a sense it was a form of humor that would cause people to laugh at my misbehavior. I was deeply addicted to misbehavior. Addictions are curable with forgiveness. Especially when the one who misbehaves reverses his or her behavior.

Here's an illustrative metaphor....

I call it a "Place of Balance." The genesis of that terminology is revealed in what I write. Its meaning can be interpreted from the consideration of a view of two stones being dropped in a calm pond and then watching the ripples. The first view is watching them proceed outward, the second a reversal of the process. Push out—push back. This I see as a life process. Pushing out is making mistakes. Pushing back is forgiving them. The meaning of their direction is the intention of the stones to find a place of balance.

It is a process much like life. A two-way street to a place of the comfort of balance. Where you have been tells you where to go. We all travel that street. We can reverse that process. Where you have been reveals direction. If you can reverse it, (push back) you can get closer to a place of comfort. These stories are told in that form of reference. They are about push out and push back. We serve each other through that process. That is what service is about. That is life.

Service means we are here to help each other. That is our way of being forgiven—by forgiving. No matter what, it can happen. It takes reversal of direction. Stories of service contain those elements. The stories I have written here are done in that vein. Service wears many hats. Not all service is *front line*. Neither are all these stories, but each one contains forgiveness.

In the summer of 2017, Steve McAlpin and I spent the better part of July in Europe revisiting the places of trauma in our past. Steve was in Bosnia in 1992; I was in France, Germany, and Austria in 1945. In a sense it was a tour of reconciliation. A tour that would enable us to reconcile in our brains the causes and purposes of our sense of discomfort, or find what one might call peace of mind. Release memories of trouble that haunt and linger, absorb the changes for the better.

Wartime combat is loaded with those memories. They never leave. They can only be healed by revisiting and amending their content. That amendment is what might be called forgiveness. Storytelling and humor are the instruments of that kind of healing. They are its descriptors. They clean and repair the muck and damage. Some of my memories are written in the following stories. Steve is involved with writing his own. We both are writing these stories in the Rochester Veteran's Writing Group. That's what this book is about.

April 1945–July 2017

Stories are about relationships. Relationships define life. Here are some related stories. All taking place over time intervals. Stories about power. The power of shooting (pushing out), and forgiveness (pushing back).

April 30, 1945 – A Day of Miracles

A memorable day for me and for the world. Funny how those things happen. There must be a reason somewhere out there. For the world it was the last miserable day of a man who had nearly destroyed what was good in it. He and his new wife, Eva Braun, were cowering in an underground bunker in Berlin, while the remnants of those who defended them were desperately trying to ward off an army of those who they had attempted to conquer and enslave. Eva and Adolf's day ended in a self-imposed tragic demise. What they had dished out, now did them in, in gunfire. This time they shot themselves—poetic justice. The symbolic head of evil had left for another place and was lost forever.

Miracle 1...

About 300 miles south of Berlin, in the eastern reaches of Bavaria, another version of push out and push in was occurring.

A task force consisting of a fleet of half-tracks of A Company, 59th Armored Infantry Battalion of the 13th Armored Division, coupled with four Sherman tanks of the 24th Tank Battalion was proceeding on a course toward capturing the Austrian city of Vienna—a large city like Berlin, and a capital as well.

World War II

Our Halftrack on the road to Vienna

The objective at that closing stage of the war was to clear out any remaining defenders who could prolong the war if they could reach the difficult-to-conquer Alps mountain range in Austria. Our task force had been making record-breaking strides in pursuit of the now-weakened remnants of Hitler's once powerful Wehrmacht.

It was not altogether a piece of cake, as last-ditch engagements were a daily occurrence. Some of those were quite deadly, and we lost many of our friends in what should have been a surrender, albeit the Spector of Hitler's wrath.

On that very same day, as our task force was approaching the Austrian border, we were confronted by a small Wehrmacht detachment defending a roadblock they had established. I don't remember all the details, but the long and short of it was that they, as a group, when confronted by our group, decided to surrender.

Being on the move, as we were, we had no way to attend to prisoners. In his wisdom, my company commander, Captain Thomas Ford, contacted via radio, the 80th Infantry Division that was following us in mop-up duty, to secure their assistance in handling our prisoners. He was advised to have someone leave the taskforce and travel back down unknown roads with about 20 German prisoners in tow to make junction with advance elements of the 80th Division to our rear. A daunting task to say the least, as this was still enemy country. Unknown roads. Hostile forces and roadblocks scattered about. Dismal cold weather. Not a situation with anything supportive in the vicinity. As luck would have it, the half-track I was in was the closest to the front of our task force. It was the same one our First Sergeant Ed Lyons approached with this latest assignment.

Sergeant Lyons, who was Captain Ford's messenger, came immediately to our half-track and asked for a volunteer to take the prisoners back to the 80th Division. Please understand that there is no set order or background experience for this kind of task, and the possibilities for disaster are enormous. That's why we were given the opportunity of volunteering.

Having been, in my past performances in his sight, more trouble than anyone else in our group, I knew I would ultimately be chosen, I decided that I might as well take it on voluntarily. So, volunteer I did, and believe me, I had difficulty in hearing myself say: "I'll do it."

Our group had been advancing very fast, through the disorganized German forces. It is my belief that they let us go by because of all the tanks and armored vehicles we had. Being a lone rifleman in the middle of that hostile environment was another story. It would take a lot of miracles to get that job done and get back to my task force.

Sergeant Lyons told me that he and Captain Ford had been in radio contact with a responsible counterpart in the 80th Infantry Division and that the route I would take would get me there. Being of the believing nature I was, I accepted that this would be a straightforward task, albeit dangerous. Lyons told me that if I backtracked the narrow mud road we were on for about a mile and got to the paved road we were formerly on, all I had to do was go left for a short distance and there would be a barn where someone from the 80th would meet me and take the prisoners. Beyond that there were no more instructions.

Having a history of being a part of the confusion that is warfare, I, in my somewhat conflicted set of beliefs, did not give further thought to the possibility that everything would work out all right, and I could safely and quickly return to the task force. Somehow, in those circumstances the normal functions of the brain shut down, and a serenely blind faith takes over. *MEA Culpa*!

Off I went. Back down the mud road with my prisoners. Surprisingly not the least bit concerned about my vulnerability in that hostile, still-resisting enemy area. About a half hour later I got to the paved road and turned left and began my search for the barn where I could deliver my prisoners.

One mile. Two miles. Three miles—no barn anywhere in sight. My sense of reality was beginning to kick in. This isn't going to be the way it was presented to me.

Something was wrong ....

My first miracle kicked in here. Just as I was introducing myself to the possibility that this was another of my many wartime screwups, I saw in the distance a small party of three soldiers. I stopped and waited until they got close enough for me to identify them and still get away if they were the enemy.

Their helmets had no flared rims which told me they were Americans. As they came into shouting range, I hollered at the top of my voice that I was from the 13th Armored Division and was bringing captured prisoners to the 80th Infantry Division. Happily, they heard my message, recognized my non-threatening situation and hollered back their recognition.

A few minutes later our two groups met and I discovered, happily, that they were an advance scouting party of the 80th Infantry Division. A sergeant and two privates. I explained my mission to them and asked if they would take the prisoners. When they understood what I was asking, they agreed. The duty part of my task was successful, now I needed to take care of me.

I had been gone for a good two hours and was not going to go along with my prisoners to the sanctuary of the 80th Division. I wanted to get back to my task force. The outlook was not good. A lot of time had elapsed, and I had no idea where my people might be located. They could have taken any number of routes.

There are senses that kick in when you are in situations of the dangerous unknown. Wartime combat lights them up and a sort of numbness sets in that allows you to function calmly in a stressful situation. I wouldn't call it fearless, but that is one of its components, like a survival instinct. So off I went, backtracking my journey by foot.

Miracle 2...

As I was walking on the paved road in the direction of the mud road a motorbike approached. As I looked, I could make out the image of a man in a German uniform speeding toward me. Fortunately for me I recognized him as an enemy before he did me. As he approached closer to where he could recognize me, I had already had my rifle pointed at him and held up my hand for him to stop. His eyes were telling. Shock and fear were the messages.

What happened next was a blur of surprising proportion. It was over quick, no more than 10 minutes total. A lot happened. He stopped his bike in front of me and raised his hands. I could see a shoulder holstered pistol. I pointed to it. He took it out and gave it to me, handle first,

My brain had now completely kicked into survival mode and I motioned him to get off his bike. He did, and in a somewhat amazing bit of communication I was able to get him to show me how to start and make it go. I cannot to this day completely understand how that happened, but it did. When one is in survival mode, miraculous understanding comes to the fore. Mine was in overdrive.

Away I went....

Leaving my unarmed German helplessly watching as I sped back down the paved road at speeds approaching 50 miles an hour, I soon reached the mud road. That was a different issue. It had such a high crown that I slipped and fell several times. Happily, I was able to restart the bike and proceed, but ever so slowly. It was getting late in the afternoon and I was praying that my task force would stay on the mud road because I could easily follow their tracks.

About two miles up that road I found the road blocked by a huge loaded cart pulled by two huge and mean looking oxen. The bike had a large air bulb horn which I honked several times to get the farmer driving the cart to pull over and let me by. There was no room on the mud road for me to get by, and the farmer was not going to pay any attention to my honking.

Miracle 3...

Being frustrated by his ignoring my horn, I hollered out at the top of my lungs:

"GET THE HELL OFF THE ROAD!!!"

With that the farmer turned around with a look of anger that quickly turned to fear and as it was changing, he jerked the reins on his two oxen and before you could in the blink of an eye. The cart, the oxen, and the farmer were ass over appetite in the ditch. I didn't skip a beat or look back. It was now really getting late and I knew that I had to get back to my task force before dark or I might never find them.

Miracle 4...

Halleluiah!!!

Just before it got completely dark, I caught up to them. To this day you cannot convince me that there were not miracles. God was with me all the way!

On July 11, 2017 Steve and I revisited the eastern reaches of Bavaria where some of my experiences of 1945 occurred, among them what I perceived to be the paved road of my story of April 30, 1945—along the same road near where I believed those adventures happened appeared a small German tavern. We were hungry and it was about the same time of the day as in my previous miraculous story. We stopped, went in, were met by the tavern owner, attired in the typical lederhosen dress of that area.

We ordered a beer and began to chat with the owner. We were able, in our own abilities to carry on a mixed German-English conversation that enabled me to tell him of my adventures along this same road 72 years earlier. Our conversation was of a completely different nature from the earlier one with the German I met in 1945. We laughed together. I paid for what he gave us. We were comfortable with each other.

At a Tavern along the Vienna road in 2017

Circumstance, and attitude have a way of changing over time. Certainly, in this situation it was clear. The miracle here was that it had changed for the better. Whatever existed before, no longer was a problem. We sat and drank beer together with smiling faces. A sure sign of the compatibility that comes with comfort.

We put away the pistols and put beer glasses in our hands. Prosit ....

1944 ...

A great year. The tide had turned. Germany and Japan were on their way to defeat. A way to go but heading in the right direction for the successful conclusion of WWII. A year of memories for me as well.

I had just been reassigned to the 13th Armored Division after being bounced around after various Army service options. Options I had chosen that were overturned by those who were in a position to do so. I was angry, but powerless and had to buck up and reorient myself for the service assignment I was being given. It was not easy. I let my anger get in the way of my performance. I couldn't forgive those who pushed me in a direction I did not choose. I was not going to be easy to manage. It became my mantra—*Trouble*....

1944 was the year the Jeep I encountered in Ireland was made. Surprisingly, I came upon that Jeep when visiting there (of all places) with my Combat Veteran buddy, we are members of the Rochester Veterans Writing Group, as well as students at the Osher Institute at RIT (Rochester Institute of Technology). We both believe storytelling is therapeutic and it gives us the vision to go back and correct mistakes made in our lives.

In 2017 we revisited our places of European conflict to see what effect our service efforts might have produced. Croatia, Bosnia, Austria, Germany, and France were our destinations. We had then planned to relax after our main journey with a little R&R in some of the more comfortable accommodations in Ireland.

It was there as we were passing through Connemara, we visited a manufacturing outlet of the famous Connemara Green Marble. We met a Mr. Joyce, the owner. As soon as he learned I was a WWII Veteran, he excused himself and disappeared. We didn't give it a second thought, but about a half-hour later who shows up in a 1944 Willys Jeep, but Mr. Joyce.

A Willys Jeep in Ireland? How so? I was flabbergasted. Long and short of it, I couldn't wait to get my hands on it. So many memories connected with it, and here in Ireland—Wow!

Get my hands on it I did, and all my memories of driving in WWII Army vehicles came flooding back. Especially of the almost two-month stint I had driving a *6x6*—a cargo truck. It was among my most rewarding experiences in the Army. I was my own boss. I had my own schedule, my own truck, my release from boredom of hanging around waiting to be called up into the combat zone. My feeling of contribution was met by everyday going to the port of Le Havre and hauling supply cargo to inland warehouses. You would have thought that I would finally get back on the straight track to being a model soldier. That, however, was not in my behavior book at that time, and I soon found less than acceptable ways to get around the official ties that were binding me.

The 1944 Willys Jeep in Ireland in 2017

Case in point. I wanted to visit my A Company buddies in France who were beyond walking distance. I only had Sundays off on my truck driving assignment and my buddies were a four-hour walk away. Eight hours of daylight was about all we had in that winter.

Got the bright idea that me and my two other A Company truck driving buddies would sign out a truck and head over to see our friends on our day off. Having been aware in previous illicit adventures that camp and motor pool security had some vulnerability if one knew how to "play the game," I came up with a plan—sign out a truck, albeit not on official business, but who knows? A questionable reason and grounds for severe punishment if discovered. Our motives were good, our methods otherwise, but, we "meant well."

On the way I almost lost the truck on a mud slicked curve on a steep hill. A close call. If I hadn't done what exactly needed to be done—disaster, maybe even our demise. A few days later, after our adventure, there was word that our escapade had reached the ears of those who meted out punishment and we were going to be called upon for an explanation.

As so often happened in my Army career, just when I was about to get burnt, I got pulled from the fire. I was rescued by a more important duty. My A Company was heading for the combat zone. Truck driving close calls looked small when looking at being sent to the mother of all close calls (if you were lucky). I must have been one of the original lucky ones. I survived. Close calls, yes. Disaster, no. Punishments, some *yes* and some *no*. Mostly *no*, Thank You God ....

The 1944 Jeep took me back. Back to places where revisiting them became my way of reconciling the trauma of their disastrous moments and events. Some of those or their effects I will describe in the next stories and many more to come on the website: *Relighting Us*. They will be found in the section called: *Veteran's Echoes*. There will be many other veterans' stories there as well. Many people are discovering storytelling to be a road to a place of comfort. A place of healing.

2017 ...

Another time, another place, different people, same connections ....

This is a story that completes the message I have been trying to send. It happened on July 13, 2017 in Luneville, France.

How come Luneville? Yes, I even asked myself the same question. But life takes strange and unexpected turns. These turns are challenges for us to use the brain we were given to unravel the twists and knots of life. You know, the ones that get so tangled that we wander about in state of confused bewilderment and look for answers in all the wrong places.

We devote ourselves to a science that attempts to reveal substance. A substance that is unreliably defined. Think of a dog chasing his tail. He never connects with it because he is moving it away from him and is not in the place where he sees it. The closest we can ever get to exactness is in likeness. Being *like* something is the only mode of definition that is achievable.

Stories have that quality of definition and perception. In stories are likenesses. In these related stories the defining element is forgiveness. Stories have a component of forgiveness. Forgiveness is what we do when we want to achieve peace. To participate in war, it is the only justifiable objective.

World War II gave us (and all the world) a good opportunity to find out what we liked and how to recognize and act on it. When I was in Eastern France and Germany in 1945, I saw disaster and separation. Man-made disaster. When I returned to those areas in 2017, I saw correction and recovery—*man-made*.

There are reasons for those differences. These stories are my attempt to set forth a look at those reasons. A look to encourage and exemplify the positive changes I saw. We can do things that harm us, and we can do things that help us. We can do that by encountering, facilitating, and supporting. Supporting is the key ingredient. Support is not unilateral; it is conditional and based on cooperation and connection.

In the first sentence of this story I used the word *connection*. Let me sketch an ordinarily hidden view of connection. By that I mean connection as found in the word "like." Each of those stories has "like" in it. See if you can pick out what is found in each story. The "like" in it, if you will. This series of stories would appear to be unrelated, but it has "like" written all over it. My Irish-descended father would use the expression: "Tis the likes of me that knows the likes of you," when reprimanding me for one of my transgressions.

So, this story has some "likes" in it, as do the others in this series. It is part of the stories of what happened in the vicinity of Luneville, France, that ultimately defined Steve's and my European trip. It is difficult for me to find the right words to express their magnitude. But, a huge nagging question in the back of my mind haunted me as to why a 92-year-old man would take such a daunting trip in the first place. And, even more perplexing, who would want to be a partner in such a venture. I couldn't really get a grasp on all of it until that warm pleasant day in Eastern France. The amazing part of it all was that I didn't even want to go to Luneville in the first place.

My original interest in that area was focused on finding a very small village nearby where 72 years ago, I had an innocent, but poignant affair with a young woman which was interrupted by circumstance. My need was to go back and explain to her why I left town so quickly without her knowing the reason. It was not any love affair, but just something that always haunted me in the sense that something was left mysteriously undone. Maybe I was just curious to see how things turned out with her, or maybe just curious, who knows? But, as with unfinished business, questions remained. That story follows.

World War II

I relied on my partner Steve to do the detail work involved in traveling on the cheap. As a former field grade Army Officer, he filled in the necessary detail gaps in my normally disorganized behavior. Further, I hadn't really given much thought to Steve's reasons for going on this somewhat unusual trip. This was no vacation or sightseeing trip. This trip had a different set of purposes. It was aimed at going back to revisit places where we took part in momentous events, to see what things might be like now—better, or worse?

Well, our stories do bring out some of that change. Most of it heading in a positive direction, as documented in earlier accounts of our visitations. July 13, 2017 was a game-changer. The next story looks at the reasons why. That story was inspired and photographically illustrated by a man and wife, named Andrew and Christa Wakeford. Andrew and Christa had no knowledge of who I was, or what I was about, except that I was a combat Veteran of WWII, and was retracing my steps of 72 years ago with another combat veteran of Afghanistan and Bosnia wars, Steve McAlpin. That was good enough for them to welcome me and share precious solid elements and stories of combat veterans. Their career lives revolved around that kind of sharing. Steve was one of the combat veterans they had interviewed, photographed, and featured in a book published by the National Geographic Society entitled: "Veteran's Voices."

The Veteran's Voices book was a publication of the National Geographic Society and a companion piece to an earlier book titled: "Portraits of Service," and published by Patton Publishing, a publishing firm owned by the Granddaughter of General George S. Patton, Jr., Commanding General of the US Third Army in Europe in which the 13th Armored Division served in the last days of WWII. In the publication "Portraits of Service," Andrew and Christa had described the friendship bond of two former enemies. A very expressive photograph of two former enemies was the basis of the whole story. A story of forgiveness and reconciliation.

Christa, Steve, Andrew, and me. July 13, 2017, Luneville, France

With all this coming together right in front of me that day, my mind was reeling. I knew that something bigger than I had planned was unfolding in front of my eyes. This stuff doesn't happen by chance. Our trip had more to it than expected. Besides, Andrew communicated to me his assessment of Steve. I cannot locate his exact words, but my memory tells me he knew Steve and would be in some form of communication with him more than what was reported in "Veteran's Voices."

Prophetic, to be sure, as our meeting in Luneville turned out. I had no idea what was in Steve's mind when he set up the lunch date as part of our trip. It was a game-changer. Our trip now became a mission.

A mission that would cry out: "What's happening here could change the world." A clear demonstration of how the world could become if we listened to "Veteran's Voices."

Combat veterans have a deep understanding of how important it is to "have your buddy's back." That understanding is paramount to understanding life. Life in all forms. Family life. Nation's relationships. It is basic to our survival—that basic. As we saw on our trip, France and Germany were now graced with open borders. We were seeing green in the fields, order and beauty in the structures where people lived and gathered. The contrast was like that of a black and white movie to one in color. The peace of forgiveness had changed to a world for the better.

More importantly, we saw an opportunity to spread the messages contained in "Veteran's Voices." I, along with my daughter Patty, had been working over the past few years on establishing a website called: "Relighting Us." It was established to give people opportunities to tell the kinds of stories that were being heard through "Veteran's Voices."

In addition to messages of forgiveness, Veteran's Voices have many bridge-building elements. Steve and I saw many rebuilt bridges in France and Germany. We came away from that lunch meeting with a fired-up expectation that we *do* have ways to make a better world. We saw it in front of our eyes. Eyes that recognized the power of forgiveness and connection. We are all brothers and sisters. A monumental lunch!

July 13, 2017 ...

The Memory of Emelienne...

The sentiment of powder and lace
Take me back to a tender place
Where memories will replace
A forgotten face
An empty space

A story of an amazing revisit to a small French village in the Province of Lorraine. A revisit in a series of life-changing adventures of my 13th Armored Division experiences of WWII.

Ever wonder why memories never leave your mind? In my view, it is because they are you. They are your accomplishments. They are your story. If something undone or traumatic lingers, it must be completed or brought to justice. Let me set the stage for this story by summarizing an earlier recollection as taken from my previously written (2005) WWII memoirs.

A Company arrived in Fremenil, Lorraine, in late March 1945, after an exhausting and frigid truck ride from Normandy. We were billeted in the several connected houses of the village. Our squad was next to a similar one on our left where a family of four lived. Father, mother, son and daughter. The son was a recently returned Maquis (Free French Armed Forces), and the daughter, a pretty blonde frizzy-headed girl of sixteen.

Because of my ability to speak some French, I quickly won the attention of the daughter. Her name was Emelienne (in my earlier account I had wrongfully named her Angelique). I must have impressed her quite a bit, because she was most willing to be in my company as much as possible. After we were there about six days, we were going to be treated to some beer and pretzels, and a movie was going to be shown on a nearby outdoor wall. I asked Emelienne to attend the movie with me, and she accepted. Here's where the story gets interesting.

That night I went to the door and knocked. I thought all there would be to it was our short walk to the movie. Surprise! Surprise! When the door opened it was her father, not Emelienne, who appeared. He was dressed in his only suit (these people were poor). Looking further into the room I saw her mother—dressed in her only formal dress. That struck me funny, but I still didn't get it until I saw Emelienne.

There she was. All powdered. coiffed, and laced in a most beautiful formal dress. I hardly recognized her. She was beautiful.

What was going on here? I'm just taking a girl to a movie being shown on a wall.

What's with the fancy dresses and suits?

It was soon apparent that mom and pop were coming along, too. Nothing spoken, but I got the message. OK, not what I had expected, but something I had to accept.

So, off we started to the movie. We had taken only a few steps when my platoon sergeant spotted me and yelled: "Hey, Whelan, get your gear and mount up, we're leaving. Right now!" In my usual way, I was mostly absent when word came down. It happened again this time, as I was throughout my entire Army career, involved in pursuing a different path in a different place. Not a model soldier....

So, without fanfare or any other form of departure, I left Emelienne and her parents, hustled back to where my equipment was, gathered it together and made for a waiting truck. Emelienne and her parents were stunned. They loudly protested, but to no avail. We were gone in a New-York minute.

A few days later when we were awaiting our combat assignment, we had assembled at the German city of Zweibrucken, my platoon sergeant, Eldon Miller, was explaining to my First Sergeant Ed Lyons why I was late for mounting the truck in Fremenil. In the conversation, Lyons said: "Whelan was damn lucky. In that part of the world, asking the girl to go to the movies is like asking for her hand in marriage—or at least an engagement."

That statement stuck in my mind for many years. So much so that it was prominent among my reasons for going back to Europe. I had to go back, find her and apologize to the pretty girl, if she were still living. I had no idea then of what I was doing. Or, at the least, tell it to her remaining family. It became a priority item on my bucket list. One of many in my series of WWII revisiting issues.

Fast forward to July 12th and 13th of 2017. Steve and I were booked to stay at a bed and breakfast location in Strasbourg, France on those dates. Our mission on this trip was to attempt to return to nearby Fremenil and revisit the scene just described. We had no clue as to where even Fremenil was located, much less finding anyone there who might have been a part of my adventures with Emelienne, and make amends.

Our hostess at the Strasbourg B&B was a charming and gracious lady named Jeanne. She treated us like brothers and went the extra mile in all directions for us, including providing a wonderful breakfast before we left on our search. Not only did she treat us so generously, but she, through the use of her computer, was able to locate the exact spot where Fremenil could be found.

And find it we did, in itself an unbelievable task, but with help of Jeanne we accomplished it. Found the exact houses involved in the story, and even the daughters and son in law of Emelienne. His name was Jean Paul, theirs were Marie and Josette.

Such excitement! The daughters scurried about their houses and came back with boxes of pictures. Sadly, Emelienne had died a few years ago, and was not able to participate in this reunion, but her offspring were there and appreciative of this moment.

I was able to recount my encounter with their mother, and a most memorable time was had that sunny afternoon. Emelienne lives on, as do all our good memories. Memories that, if revisited, allow us to redeem what needs redemption, and enjoy again, what was enjoyed.

A photo of Emelienne and her family (daughters in front row probably taken around the 1960's Emelienne is in the center)

In every way, this experience was far beyond my expectations. It even had elements in it that Steve and I shall recall in others of these continuing stories. Another story of revisiting the past to rectify it. There is a comfortable healing of the effects of the guilt of unfulfillment.

Our humanity lives on forgiveness when we are hurt or are in pain. Separation is the ultimate source of pain. Aunt Jackie taught me forgiveness. We all "mean well," but, must learn from each other if we want to attain comfort. Stories can help get us there. Stories of service help me get it back together. I am beginning to heal. Thanks to all involved for their service....

A Small Addendum.

Honor, in my view, reflects forgiveness. Andrew and Christa Wakeford are so dedicated. They honor veterans who served their people. I appreciate their honoring, especially as I am from the generation of their parents. What a legacy they have inherited and share. Andrew of British parents and Christa of German, who fought against each other in WWII. Their work is much appreciated by all. May we emulate their devotion. Truly, "mean well."

Josette, Marie (daughters) and Jean Paul (son in law) with me at left, 2017

Sausages Anyone?

Robert (Bob) Whelan

It was late April, 1945. Two weeks earlier we had joined Patton's Third Army as it pushed through what was left of the German resistance. The war was almost over. The 13th Armored Division was on the road to our last objective—Vienna. We were moving so fast we had to stop and let our supply trains catch up to us so we could get restocked with food, ammunition, water, gasoline, and all the supplies we needed. We stopped for two days to get refreshed and restocked.

Plattling—City Center 2017

No matter where we were, or what we were doing, we had lots of continuing adventures, some on the humorous side. This one happened in more than one setting and incorporating the same kind of dualities I have been dealing with in all these writings. They were set in two sausage shops miles and years apart. The first one happened in late April 1945 in the small city of Plattling on the Isar River in lower southeastern Bavaria.

One of our sergeants had discovered a very large butcher shop loaded with sausages strung from the ceiling in long rows. I went in and was impressed by the large quantity and variety of all the different sausages hung there. We took a few, but our A Company Mess Sergeant, who was in the supply trains that had caught up to us, spotted them and proceeded to load them into some food storage containers he had brought with him.

In our race through what was left of Germany, we were getting quite accustomed to "living off the land." Army rations were at the best terrible, and good food we could lay our hands on became one of the ways to make our misery more enjoyable. We were getting quite good at it. So, into the food containers went the huge quantities of sausages that hung in that sausage shop.

Racks and Racks of Delicious Sausages—The Spoils of War

Humor is poetic justice. My stories of wartime experiences are told in that vein. They are a way of inserting time into the definition of reality. What happens at one time has an influence on a similar happening at another time. It can be good or bad depending on how it is used. Good use is found in forgiveness, and bad if not. This story is the model for my other war service stories. There is forgiveness over time if you allow it to happen. See if you can find a way to laugh as this story unwinds.

Early in May 1945, our mission to take Vienna was abruptly halted by those in charge of our wartime activities. We were halted by orders from our higher authorities to stop our advance to Vienna. Stop it right at the Austrian border. A Company thus found itself stopped and billeted in a hamlet called Berg nearby the small town of Neu-Otting.

Sausage Time at Neu-Otting—May 1945

As soon as Sergeant Lillard, our mess sergeant, could get his kitchen up and running we were treated to a magnificent sausage extravaganza. What a celebration to have after a long, exhausting wartime terrible foray from one side of Germany to the other. We were getting payback for our agonies and we relished every different kind of sausage we could lay our hands on that Lillard's feast.

War is not pretty. It is not kind, but if it leads to forgiveness it has created a good. This is where humor comes in. It can play the sympathetic role of forgiveness. Laughter and oneness come together as expression of its power. Laughter is antidote to anger. It unties the knots that bind us. Here's where laughter enters this continuing story (all earthly stories continue until we depart this earth).

Fast forward to May 1951 ....

I was working as a buyer trainee at the J. N. Adam Co., Buffalo, New York. I lived on the east side of town and always traveled to work on one of the main thoroughfares from that part of town called Genesee Street. One day one of my fellow trainees told me of a brand-new sausage shop that had just opened on Genesee Street. It was opened by a newly arrived sausage maker from Germany and the sausages were worth trying. I needed no more encouragement. On my way home that very day, I stopped in the shop.

As I walked in the door, a sight overwhelmed me with a sense of déjà vu. "*Holy Cats*, this looks just like the sausage shop I helped liberate in Plattling six years ago!" I was stunned. It was so exactly like that shop. Sausages strung across the shop. Big ones, little ones, dark ones, light ones, fat ones, thin ones, on and on. It took me a minute to get my breath back. I couldn't believe what I was seeing.

As I was recovering from my reverie, the shop owner came into the shop from a door in the rear. A middle-aged man of medium build wearing an apron. He greeted me in a Germanized accent and waited for my reply. It took me a while to get back into a state of consciousness where I could address why I was there in the first place. When I did, I ordered a few sausages and took out my wallet to pay for them. I could not suppress my excitement any longer, and calmly asked him where he was from in Germany.

"Plattling" he replied. I thought: "No, this isn't happening, but I have to ask." So, I asked: "Did you have a sausage shop there in 1945?"

"Ja"

"Was it ransacked by a bunch of American Soldiers?"

"Ja"

"This *is* happening! I'm talking to the guy whose shop we ransacked."

I said: "You're looking at one of them right now." Without a blink or any outward sign, he acknowledged my confession and I thought I heard a small chuckle emitting from his voice. He was not angry or emotional in any other way than being pleasant and accommodating.

I went home. We ate the sausages. They were excellent. So much so that I went back many times and bought many more. No more was spoken of our actions in 1945, nor of his either. They were buried in the past. We had a new relationship.

Forgiveness is a two-way street....

The Healing Power of Time

Robert (Bob) Whelan

The picture below taken in late February 2019 shows two smiling faces together with a snowman in front of St. Louis Church in Pittsford, New York. The man, Bob Whelan, was, in 1945 an Armored Infantryman Private engaged as a point man for an advancing infantry company involved in capturing the small town of Opladen in one of the last great battles of WWII—The Battle of the Ruhr Pocket. The woman, Christel Rinkleff, in 1945, was a five-year old girl who lived in Opladen. She now lives in Henrietta, New York, and attends St. Louis.

In mid-April 1945, the Company I was with was involved with taking Christel's home town as our 9th US Army was advancing against 300,000 of the German Wehrmacht surrounded in the Ruhr Pocket. We were proceeding on foot against the Opladen defenders who were using every available means to stop us. As we moved up a broad meadow leading to the town, we were being bombarded with whatever the Germans could employ. It was another of the chaotic situations we were experiencing every day in that battle.

God was with me in all of this, as I had several close calls with enemy artillery and bullets. As we were getting near the town, a large turf-covered shed appeared in front of us. I had the unenviable job of point man, and served as an advanced scout to explore enemy sanctuaries and suspicious houses. My platoon leader instructed me to advance to the building, open the door and determine if there were any enemy inside. Not

World War II

an enviable task, but it had to be done, and people like me had to do it.

I quickly approached the building, stood to one side of the door, rifle in hand, ready to shoot if necessary. Thrust open the door, poked my head inside and was greeted by a screaming chorus of terror like you never heard before.

When I recovered my sensibilities, I could see in the far corner of the shed about 25 or 30 people of all descriptions huddled and shrieking at the tops of their lungs. No able-bodied men, no weapons, but, several elderlies of both sexes and about 15 children ranging from 3 to 12 huddled in a ball in the middle of that group. A sight that still lives in my mind.

In the group of adults was a young woman of about 25 years who immediately confronted me and addressed me in English that she wanted to see the person in charge of this threat. I was amazed at her cool and courageous behavior.

She so impressed me that I ran as quick as I could to find the lieutenant who sent me and have her meet with him. He came with me and assured her that we would not harm her and those inside the hut. With that she went back inside the hut and we moved on toward Opladen.

Fast forward to 2017. Christel and Bob met during activities at St. Louis Church in Pittsford. She had fallen on some ice outside a building nearby, and those of us in attendance came to her assistance. In the course of that chance meeting we became acquainted and, in our conversations, I learned Christel grew up in Opladen, and was there in April 1945 when we were involved with the incident described above.

She, at that time was only about five years old, and her memories, while horrific, were vague as to her whereabouts during that April day when we were advancing on her town. She could not recollect whether she was in the hut or not, but the terror and confusion were not forgotten. I'll never know if she was one of those children huddled pitifully in the far corner, but the vision still lingers in my memory of children like her in my view. We'll never know, but I can fully understand what they were experiencing at that time.

In any event, we were in the same situation at the same time. We just had different roles in the scene. We were enemies. Opposite sides at the same place and time.

I returned to the scenes of my WWII experiences in the summer of 2017, including the town of Opladen. My partner in that journey, Steve McAlpin, a combat veteran of both Afghanistan and Bosnia wars, was with me and took a picture of a meadow near Opladen which reminded me of the one of 1945.

The biggest part of that recollection was about the difference that 70 years had made. No longer young, no longer in different places. Places that had changed over time. Places that had changed from rejection to acceptance. We were together and at peace.

This picture was taken in 1945, a short time after the battle of the Ruhr Pocket, as we were in the process of leaving Germany to come home and get ready to fight the Japanese. I am standing in the right-hand doorway.

The Snow Man

Robert (Bob) Whelan

In the previous story an important component was the setting of the 2019 connection. In this case, the snowman in the front of St. Louis Church in Pittsford. It too, has a humorous side.
In February of 2019 a group of parishioners, with the blessings of their priests, built a huge snowman smack dab in front of their church for all to see.

A statement of the beauty by taking what was considered by many burdensome and unwelcome and transforming it into something in keeping with the purpose of the church— shaping it into the image of a smiling person. Complete with the ashes of the Ash Wednesday celebration on its forehead.

There you have it. Lots of happy images in that snowman. A fitting background for a deep understanding of connection, humor, and its companion, forgiveness.

A giant snowman in front of St. Louis Church in Pittsford has ashes on its forehead for Lent. JOYCE ARNS

Note: *The fame of the Snowman has been spread by the Democrat & Chronicle. He has become recognized as a symbol of connection in Rochester. In effect, a true "Spirit of Rochester."*

Just Briggin' Soldiers

Anonymous

Once upon the end of World War II in Europe there were these two infantrymen, whom we shall randomly name "Bob" and "Kurt." Here those two find themselves on some long-forgotten oceanic dock in western Europe recently built up by a Navy construction battalion—*Seabees*—to ferry military supplies in, and soldiers back out, more or less from & to the United States. The war in Europe had just been successfully ended, more or less, and many, many U.S. troops needed ferrying back. Some of those rode 1st-to-3rd class on a Navy ship, passenger class depending really only on a soldier's name arranged alphabetically—Army logic. And some of them rode *jailbird class*. Bob returned home in that last one.

Bob claims that he remembers little about the circumstances which landed him in that lower part of the transport ship, but it likely had to do with some kind of lunch beverage, and some kind of Army officer who got the receiving end of one of Bob's verbal paragraphs a week earlier. Now, Bob's natural congenial temperament would not particularly make something like that happen, but somehow it did. Did I use the word *Irish*? They say that a fist was involved also, but the case paperwork from back then did not survive until today. I mean, what the heck? The war had just ended! The Services sometimes have no sense of humor!

Well, *somebody* had to make the painful arrest and detention of various Bob-type soldiers, so here comes Kurt, the newly appointed TEMPORARY M.P..... The Army needed a few extra

TEMPORARY M.P.s for dockside duty, so the Army used the usual scientific method of assigning appropriate jobs to appropriately trained soldiers: "You, you, and you!" Those *You's* consisted of the first individuals on the right scene at the really wrong time, and who couldn't get their nametags out of sight fast enough. What the heck? The war just ended, and who needs to move fast anymore! Nevertheless, some M.P. officer caught Kurt's name and service record details, and decided that, "Here is a good law-&-order name!" Did I say *German*?

Anyway, here's the likely story about *temporary* M.P. Kurt escorting Prisoner Bob to dockside, then below to the ship's brig. We have to fill in the conversation between the two, though we can guess it pretty well:

TEMPORARY M.P. KURT: *What the #*≢&€Ø!! 're they sending you back this way for?*

PRISONER BOB: *#*≢&€Ø!! if I know! I did pretty good in Germany, and now this!*

TEMPORARY M.P. KURT: *Well, I was in #*≢&€Ø!! Italy, four #*≢&€Ø!!years, and now this. #*≢&€Ø!!*

PRISONER BOB: *Yeah, what da' #*≢&€Ø!!. We gotta' do what they say we gotta' do.*

TEMPORARY M.P. KURT: *#*≢&€Ø!! right. Whad'dya'do, hit an officer?*

PRISONER BOB: *[cough][pause]. Uh, not really. I think a #*≢&€Ø!! chair got in the way, or something……… and I hear they might reschedule us to the #*≢&€Ø!!Pacific now.*

TEMPORARY M.P. KURT: *Pacific?!!! #*≢&€Ø!!#$!#*≢&€Ø!! Ø≢#!! #$!#*≢&€Ø!! !!*

PRISONER BOB: *Yeah, well who the #*≢&€Ø!! knows…?*

TEMPORARY M.P. KURT: *Ya' know, last month I did the exact same thing you just did, but they didn't stockade me. Here I am, and here you #*≢&€Ø!! are...but who's this coming now?*

SHIP'S "CAPTAIN," ENSIGN WHATSHISNAME: [entering] *Down below, gentlemen! I'll say, "To the brig," and d'you all know where that came from? Back long ago the navies kept prisoners in retired twin-mast sailing ships—brigs—and the name stuck. That's why prisoners in the brigs got called "brigands."*

Prisoner Bob muttered something like, "My, that's interesting, you s____b____ pompous #*≢&€Ø!! old officer-grade poop!"

TEMPORARY M.P. Kurt, mindful that the positions of him and his escort could easily have been switched, chatted lightly to PRISONER BOB, "You know, if you were a general, they wouldn't put you in this brig. They don't want no *brigand general* here."

Prisoner Bob, warming to the conversation, puffed, "I ain't no *briggin'* general, I'm a *briggin'* private!"

The only excellent news here is that those two long-serving infantrymen never did end up on a Pacific-bound, Japanese-campaign ship. But what the heck? Their war, well-served, had just ended!

When's the next bar stop?

If you happen to run into either of these two named good soldiers, both will deny every word of this. Don't believe them!

KOREAN WAR AND PRE-VIETNAM

Jake–From the Grave

Charles F. Willard

Pieced together from conversations with Evelyn Farrell

The only time I ever cried was when your Mama died. I took some petals from the roses and dried them. I put them in my billfold. I had them 'til I died. I loved that woman. If I'd had a mother like yours, I wouldn't have made all the rotten choices I did in my life. I would have been a better person.

When my Ma died, I never shed a tear. Not one tear. You were the one who cried.

She was cremated. When they called and said, "Come get the ashes," I told 'em, "We'll pick them up when we can get there." What was I going to do with those damn ashes? She was nothin' but hell to live with when I was growing up. Later on, too. I'm not gonna say "I'm glad she's dead." What I'm gonna say is, "Now we can get on with our life, and we can have a life...."

I was born in '31, in the Great Depression. Dad was a sometime actor. You can imagine how much money that brought in during those times. So, he found odd jobs and factory work here and there. We never had much, but Pa treated me right. He was a swell guy, but kinda' ineffectual, you know? It was Ma who ruled the roost.

Ma said her getting pregnant with me was the worst thing that ever happened to her. Ruined her career. Ruined her life. She was a would-be dancer. (She never had any sort of a career to ruin, I found out, later). But she threw that in my face every day. "If it wasn't for you, Irving," she always called me

Irving just to make me mad, I guess, "I would have been a star, a big star. Maybe I could have danced with Fred Astaire, or Gene Kelly. Maybe I would have been in the movies, if it wasn't for you."

A kid listens to that crap every day and it does stuff to him. By the time I was seventeen, I was a mean, mouthy smartass. Know how I got kicked out of school?

There was this teacher we hated. She didn't take our sass, so we showed her. Me and a couple of the other kids came up with the idea. We made her some fudge. Put lots of ex-lax in it. Made her sick, you bet. She was out of school for a week. 'Course, they found out about it. Traced it back to us, so out we went, on our asses.

There I was, seventeen, no diploma, no job. Bummed around in construction for a year or so, didn't like it much. They gave us orders. Made us do things their way. It was hard work. Too hard for a person of my elevated standing. Me and another kid talked it over, figured we'd make hot-shit commandos. So we chucked the construction work, went down to the recruiting office and joined the Marines.

Let me tell you, the Marines gave me the biggest whipping I ever had. They ground that smart-ass kid down to a whimpering heap of nothing, then took that pile of garbage and forged it into some sort of a man. Whatever I've done right in my life, I owe to the grit they put in my spine and the respect they made me feel for others.

One Sunday morning, I was lying on my bunk listening to the radio. They interrupted the music with a bulletin that the North Koreans had invaded the South. It was June 25, 1950. Truman wasn't gonna let that stand, and within a few weeks our unit was shipped out. By the time we got to Korea, in August of 1950, the "People's Army" had driven the UN forces all the way down into the Pusan Perimeter at the very south end of Korea. We found ourselves in a fight to the death until old MacArthur pulled off that landing at Inchon Harbor and we began to whip their asses all the way back into the North.

We rolled those commies up like a worn-out carpet until we were nearly to the Yalu River—that's the border between North Korea and China. It was November, and freezing cold in those mountains. We rested for a day there, to celebrate in the snow with a warm Thanksgiving meal. Turkey and all the trimmings. Relax. Rejoice. We won. We'd be home for Christmas.

Hah! In a couple days, as we made what we thought was the final drive to the Yalu, masses of Chinese streamed across that river and caught us flat-footed. Surprised, surrounded and way outnumbered, we panicked. You couldn't call it a retreat. The whole damn thing disintegrated into a demoralized, disorganized run-away. It was a scrambling, confused catastrophe, with thousands wounded and killed. They went home for Christmas, all right. Just not the way they expected.

They say that was the worst military fiasco for American troops in the whole of the twentieth century. In less than a month, those commie bastards drove us all the way back into South Korea.

"War is hell" but that don't tell the half of it. Growing up was hell. War is a hell of a lot worse than hell.

Cold. Colder than I've ever been. Relentless below-zero cold. Night or day, no way to get warm. Fear. Constant the whole time, because there were no battle lines. We never knew where the enemy was. Ahead? Behind? Around the next bend, waiting in the trees? Cold and fear. They paralyze the brain and body. Things don't work.

Korean War and Pre-Vietnam

Desperate. Stumbling, half running, down through those mountains on frozen feet. Rough, impossible ground, deep, icy, treacherous snow. Frozen hands, can't hold the rifle. It disappears in a drift. Can't stop. Teeth chatter. Body shakes and shivers like a nonstop seizure. Breath comes in gasps and sobs from fright and exertion. Artillery bursts too close, splatters frozen mud, blood and body parts. Gunfire. Men fall, scream and die. Run. Run like hell. Got to get away.

Me and Arthur, my black buddy, scramble arm-in-arm, try to keep each other upright. The blasts get closer. Find cover, any cover as the dusk deepens, refuge from the onrushing enemy and the driving snow. The cold cuts through us like a scythe. Ahead, we see a huge, jagged shell hole, half filled with clods of rock and dirt, intermingled with half-dismembered corpses. Shadowy, rigid limbs jut at odd angles in the blowing, drifting murk. Quick. Into that pit. Burrow underneath the bodies and the dirt. Maybe the Gooks'll pass us by.

Exhausted, we lie there between the frozen ground and the freezing cadavers, no way to stem the shivering and the revulsion. We hear them above us. The rumble of the tanks and trucks. The guttural, sing-song Chinese chatter. Too close. Will they find us? The night lasts forever. Our arms and bodies wrapped around each other for warmth and reassurance, Arthur keeps me sane, whispering in my ear. I hope I do the same for him. Battle begets trust and tolerance, and respect.

I only prayed once in my life, and it was that night. "Lord, if you get me out of this, if you let me live, I'll never complain about anything again."

We made it, somehow. Fifty-some thousand didn't, in that forgotten war.

I went on to live my life. Got out of the Marines, after a while, when Ma wrote and said Pa was dying, that I had to come home and take care of him—and her. Stuck around after that for a while, but couldn't find a decent job, so I re-upped, this time in the Air Force. A peacetime gig now. Like a country club after the Marines and Korea.

Had some AP duty, so when I got out, I took a job with the Tampa police. Did that for a while then switched to fire fighting. Rough duty, but better than the crap you have to take when you're a cop.

Made some investments along the way, and some marriages. Investments worked out, the marriages didn't, until I met Evie. She told me, "The divorces are over. You're stuck with me until I bury you."

We had a great time, traveling the country in our RV. Then her grandkids were born. Holding that first baby, I didn't know what to do. Then that innocent little face looked up at me, and my whole world caved in. My cold, hard heart melted. For the first time in my life, I felt real love, with a purpose other than me. I doted on those babies, being a Grandpa, spoiling them, watching them grow. God, I had fun with those little kids.

I wanted to see them get to be adults, and make sure they grew up to be better people than me. But I had to say goodbye too soon. When I got into my eighties, I got ALS—Lou Gehrig's disease. Service-induced, the VA said. Awful sickness. No cure, just watch while it sucks the life out of you. Evie, bless your heart, you took care of me till the day I died. You said I never complained.

This short story is dedicated to our three grandchildren, Cayden, Chase and McKenna. They gave Jake the priceless gift of unconditional love.

—*Evelyn Farrell*

Ike's Skysweepers

Vaughn Stelzenmuller

President Dwight D. (Ike) Eisenhower, That Is

While scrummaging through some old boxes of "stuff," I ran across something really great. Here was this 4X6 black & white photo of my Uncle Pinkney (Pink) Jackson in mid-1950s Army uniform.

Standing there in B&W print, this Army *hunk* in pressed fatigues and "Ridgway" cap, stood my very own between-the-wars Uncle Pink! Beside the fact that I never looked that good, in *or* out of uniform, I wondered what those GIs did for a military living back then. Why not ask?

To my astonishment and delight, it turns out some of my uncle's Army time revolved around training to deploy and fire the M51 "Skysweeper" 75mm antiaircraft gun. That baby was the Army's stopgap measure just before introducing the Nike air defense missile system. What a wonderful boyhood '50s memory, not only of the Nike missile demonstrations on TV—how could you miss those—but also newsreels of the M51 being fired. The huge gun was semiautomatic! *Fan-tastic*! These giant shells fired at about 1-1/2 second intervals, and even more fabulous, the gun mounted a small target-tracking radar system! To this young '50s boy watching, I truly believed that the radar transmitter would "fix" an enemy jet in its sights, and shoot the bad guy down like popping a plastic duck in an old-fashioned shooting gallery.

Not so. To operate this complicated equipment, much training would be needed. From what Uncle Pink told me, the gun must have been so complicated that the regular GIs didn't get much chance to touch it, much less shoot it. How fun it would have been, he said, to just tow the thing to some woods and hunt squirrels! I don't think his buddies would have wanted to pay for that huge ammo, though. It's very likely that in an emergency, the first M51s would have been hastily deployed around large U.S. cities, and would have initially been operated by senior noncommissioned officers.

Today it's easy to see why serving the M51 (and the country) then would have been a really tough job. And dire. That "fabulous" little radar tracker would likely allow only 30 seconds of outgoing Skysweeper antiaircraft fire, after which time the enemy aircraft would track the gun's radar signal straight back to the gun crew. Jet-mounted missiles weren't nearly as accurate as today's, but the M51 didn't look very mobile either, so moving out of the way of repeated enemy jet aircraft return fire would have been impossible.

Here's where the lower-ranking GIs, like Uncle Pink, would come in. Namely, a day after the first senior crews had been destroyed. This, friends, would have been a horrible direct order for any young soldier to get.

But doesn't this point out why military service was crucial during the time between Korea and Vietnam?

Interestingly, this public demonstration of the M51 may have been one of the very few times that *any* GIs actually got to live-fire the gun! My uncle tells me that they didn't really get much literal hands-on-the-gun time at Fort Bliss, Texas.

What was his rank during his service time? With laughter, Uncle Pink told me he didn't think he *had* a rank—"PFC, or something." Of course.

Now, doesn't this point out a *neglect,* and a *problem*? We have largely *neglected* the fact that a million-plus Service people during the middle 1950s-60s filled huge military gaps to keep the United States defensively strong. Not only for the U.S., but obviously we protected the entire free world at that time from that other ugly part of the world, considerably less free, and much more aggressive. The neglect of respect for those gaps which Service persons filled is the *problem* part.

Our GIs and sailors may have chuckled and tsk-tsk'ed about their vulnerabilities (like Ike's Skysweepers), but that's beside the point. The fact that *real* persons had signed up to man those vulnerable equipment systems means something. No, it means much more than that. Many of these persons had been drafted, as the Selective Service Act was quite active then. They *had* to be there, and they served. Don't let their joking and *pooh-poohing* of the experience mislead you. We honor them just as strongly.

Pinkney S. Jackson, Ford, and Ft. Bliss

Veterans, Our Grandfathers

Michael John Lemke

On Memorial Day 2007 I was granted the high honor of sitting with the Korean War veterans in front of their monument at the service in Colorado Springs at Memorial Park. Before the service began I met them and their surviving wives. I have not the words to *properly* address their impact on me on that solemn day of recognition of all our fallen brothers and sisters, and the families they left behind. Still, I will attempt to put something down:

It was not merely their limitless hospitality, their absolute dignity, their distinguished uniforms and careers.

It was not the fact that they are the remaining element of the most forgotten war in our nation's modern history.

It was not that they insisted I stand with them, as the wreath was laid at their granite memorial, and I tried to remain seated, as I had not fought in their conflict.

It was not the total humility they demonstrated by thanking me for my service, which was not as long or difficult as theirs.

It was not just the well of my emotions I had while wearing my uniform from Iraq for the first time in four years.

It was not simply the tiny Girl Scout giving me her handmade card and thanking me for my service, indeed, reminding me of my own daughter, whom I love dearly. You must understand, it was a Girl Scout who handed me a flag on the day I departed for war, who told me she would pray for my safe return.

It was because of these Korean War veterans and their invite that I was finally, truly home for this day!

My fellow Americans, these men are the country's Grandfathers, the wise sages, mentors to whom we must listen.

For it is they who have forgotten more than we will ever know! They model all that we should be and do.

To all the Korean veterans who may read this: I stand in your shadow, and pray to the God of my meager understanding, that I shall at the time of my death, have lived a life as worthy, selfless, and sacrificing as yours. Enjoy heaven, and put in a good word for me please (because I know you will be heard there); I know you have seen hell.

VIETNAM

Flying the T-37

Charles F. Willard

Cessna T-37B Dragonfly (better known as "Tweetybird") shown against the backdrop of the Superstition Mountains, Williams AFB, AZ

One month out of Syracuse University, with a brand-new second lieutenant's commission from ROTC, a ten-day cross-country drive deposited me at Williams Air Force Base, Arizona, fifteen miles southeast of Phoenix. The date was July 9, 1961. *Hot damn*, I was gonna be an Air Force pilot.

First, three weeks of ground school, learning all the aircraft systems and operating procedures, memorizing checklists, flight rules, base protocols. And learning about hypoxia. "Insidious from the onset." More about that later.

Vietnam

The Air Force didn't mess around. It started us right out in jets. No tame propeller-driven trainers for us. We climbed right into the T-37, the primary training jet. A pint-sized screamer, it was 7,000 *cps* of unadulterated twin jet noise pollution. Though it was tiny as Air Force craft go, sitting there on the ramp it looked like a little bundle of pent up energy.

"Your grandmother could fly this crate, so don't screw up, lieutenant." If the IP was trying to allay my first-flight trepidation, he was unsuccessful.

"We're late. We got a 1410 block time. Get your gear and let's kick the tires and light the fires."

I grabbed what I thought was my helmet from the full rack of them, each fitted to the individual student pilot, and slung my parachute over my shoulder. We double-timed to the flight line in the shimmering afternoon heat. I pulled on the thin deerskin Air Force-issue flying gloves. These came up over the wrists to protect your skin from contact with the searing-hot aluminum fuselage.

A quick but thorough preflight, the sharp eyes of my instructor insuring I missed nothing in my haste, then we buckled into our chutes and mounted the cockpit. On with the helmet. With the visor down and the oxygen mask attached, it made you look like a combination Alan Shepard/Darth Vader, oxygen breathing tube hanging down, swinging like a baby elephant trunk.

I fastened the seat belt and shoulder harness, plugged the oxygen tube into its source, coupled the radio cords so I could communicate with my instructor and the tower, ran through the engine-start checklist, and circled a gloved fist in the air, index finger extended, a signal to the crew chief, fire extinguisher at the ready, that I was about to fire up the

- 89 -

engines. Lowering the canopy against the insufferable screech of the two centrifugal engine compressors, I keyed the mike.

"Williams Tower, Smokepot 28, taxi for takeoff." Each student had his own call-sign. Cool.

"Roger, 28. Taxi Ragtop 3-1 left, wind 2-8-0 at 1-0 knots, altimeter 3-0-1-2. Cleared to taxi."

This was my first flight, a full orientation, so my instructor, sitting next to me in the side-by-side cockpit, took it from there. We climbed out to 20,000 feet. It was important to be way above the surrounding mountains, some of them stretching to nearly 9,000 feet.

Things looked way different from up here, the air so clear I could easily see over 100 miles. My IP pointed out the boundaries of the training area where we would do all our practicing for the next six months, and the key landmarks. Four Peaks to the north, Superstition Mountains to the east, Mount Lemmon way down south near Tucson, the Santans to the west.

Then the fun began. He started with the tame stuff. A lazy eight, a tight chandelle, a barrel roll, an aileron roll. These are fairly gentle exercises, pulling 2 to 3 G's.

Then a loop, an Immelmann, a Cuban eight, a clover leaf. These acrobatics can pull 4, 5, 6 G's, depending in how hard you pull back on the stick. I can feel my eyeballs rolling down into my mouth and all my blood descending toward the soles of my feet. Things go gray to black in a hurry if I don't tense the hell out of my stomach and leg muscles. All these tricks I would have to learn and become proficient at.

"Are you airsick yet?"

"No, sir!" I assured him.

"Well, let's try a couple of other little things, then."

It was well known that, on your first flight, your IP would try every violent maneuver he could think of to make you airsick. Pilots can't get airsick. Getting airsick would wash me out early, saving the Air Force beaucoup bucks in training expense.

We climbed to 24,000 feet, the service ceiling of the aircraft.

"I'll show you a spin. A spin is what happens if you stall the aircraft. The wings stop flying, and you tumble out of the air. So, it's important to know how to recover. In the T-37, it takes a few thousand feet for the spin to stabilize, and then a few more thousand feet to fly out of it, so we have to start as high as we can go. If we haven't recovered by the time we pass through 10,000 feet, we're gonna eject."

"Ej-j-ject?"

"Yep. If I say 'eject' and you say 'what?' you'll be talkin' to yerself, 'cuz I'll be gone."

He brought the throttle to idle and pulled back on the stick. The nose came up, the airspeed went toward zero and we stopped flying. The aircraft fell off on a wing and began to spin and tumble crazily. The IP pushed pro-spin rudder, pulled the stick back into his stomach and held it there. The horizon tilted, wobbled and spun as the plane rotated out of the sky. I watched the altimeter unwind through 20,000, through 18,000, through 16,000. I had my clammy hands gripped around the ejection handles. Just then the IP firewalled the stick and shoved opposite rudder. The nose dipped, the wings leveled, the plane gained airspeed and we were flying again at 14,000 feet.

"Plenty of altitude to spare. I could have flown it out earlier but I wanted to see how you'd react. You're still with us and I guess you're not gonna get airsick. Good for you. Want to try your hand now?"

"Y-you bet."

I took the stick and throttle. The aircraft handled easily, responsive to my tentative control movements. I got bolder. I would try a loop de loop. I …

… I felt a hand clap over my oxygen mask, shoving it against my face. I saw another hand flick my oxygen lever to 100%.

"Wha…?

"You passed out. Your oxygen mask wasn't tight to your face. Pull the straps as taut as you can get them. I don't think your helmet's fitting right. Enough for today. We're going home."

Back on the ground, I found that haste and first flight nerves had caused me to take the wrong, way too big helmet. If I had made the same mistake after I soloed, you would not be reading this story. Hypoxia—lack of oxygen. A sneaky and silent killer. Insidious from the onset.

Flying the T-33

Charles F. Willard

She was a cranky, crotchety old bird by the time I flew her in basic pilot training, the fleet of them about at the end of their operational life. By this time, January 1962, many of the other training bases had already transitioned to the modern, supersonic T-38 Talon, the same craft the astronauts were flying as they jetted about the country on their PR assignments.

The T-33, or T-bird (T for training), was the tandem cockpit version of America's first operational jet fighter, the P-80 Shooting Star (P for pursuit). It was designed in 1943 and saw limited action toward the end of World War II. Relabeled the F-80, (F for fighter) she held the line in Korea against the MIG-15 until the North American F-86 Saberjet became available.

She was a straight-winged, subsonic old clunker. If you put her into a dive and tried to coax her through the sound barrier, she would have none of it. She developed "aileron buzz" at about .9 Mach and refused to go any faster. Not good if you had a MiG on your tail. All you could do before he shot you down was whip the throttle to idle, throw out the speed brakes, barrel roll and hope he would overrun you and come into your gun-sights. Many a MiG bought the farm that way.

By today's standards, she was nearly primordial. As the first operational jet, she had none of today's technology. Her instrumentation was World War II vintage. You had to fly her by the seat of your pants.

She had a tricycle landing gear but no nose wheel steering. On the ground, you pointed her where you wanted her to go by gently tapping one brake or the other. This worked pretty well if you had up a head of steam, but from a standing start, if you tapped a little too hard, the nose wheel cocked itself 45 degrees to the line of travel, and you were stuck, like in the mud.

The only remedy for this was to call the tower on the radio, confess your ignominious lack of finesse for all to hear and plead for a crew chief to come uncock the wheel and get you pointed in the right direction.

Mounting the cockpit of a Lockheed T-33 on a CAVU* day

Starting her single engine was an exercise in proper sequencing. "Ignition switch on before you start the fuel flow, you idiot, or you'll blow the turbine buckets through the sides of the fuselage."

And if you shoved the throttle forward too fast, you over-temped the engine and blew the turbine buckets through the sides of the fuselage. Not good if you had a MiG on your tail and needed to get the flock out of there. Blow the canopy, fire the ejection seat, hit the silk and hope you land in friendly territory.

But the old girl was tough and reliable (more or less, for her day) and proved fairly forgiving of young student pilots' peccadillos and lapses. But like any aircraft, if you treated her badly, handled her roughly, or disrespected her idiosyncrasies, she would splatter your ashes across several acres.

A sure and steady platform under non-dog-fight conditions, she was a pleasure to fly on instruments, holding a compass heading without wandering too far, and staying close to altitude when properly trimmed. She responded to the small, swift corrections required for close formation flying and she had enough power and stability to perform all the acrobatic maneuvers with a smoothness that belied her antiquity.

She treated me well, generally. I walked away from all her landings. The last one was hairy, but not her fault. I was on my final check ride. It had gone reasonably well, to my relief, assuring, I thought, graduation from pilot training with a shiny new set of Air Force wings. I entered the pattern for the final landing. I was on course, on altitude and on airspeed, exactly where I was supposed to be.

Strangely, I noticed a flyspeck on my windscreen, directly in my line of vision. It was getting larger! Rapidly. Too rapidly. In instant panic, I realized that the now huge flyspeck was another aircraft and it was aimed directly between my eyes. With a closure rate of nearly 500 miles per hour, there was no time to think, only to react. I firewalled the stick. The huge dark shape flashed over our canopy, only inches separating us from a fiery mid-air.

My check ride instructor, in the back seat with no forward vision, had been unaware of the danger. As his head banged off the canopy, a fusillade of profanity erupted over the intercom. Shaken and stuttering, I explained what had happened and, completing the landing pattern with little of my former precision, I banged the old girl into the runway, bouncing her bones a couple of times before she settled in.

Well, the old battle-axe had responded quickly enough to save our bacon, but I was glad to be done with her and on to Sewart Air Force Base in Tennessee to learn how to fly brand new C-130's.

---

*Ceiling and visibility unlimited

Flying the C-130

Charles F. Willard

I rolled through the gates of Sewart Air Force Base outside of Smyrna, Tennessee, about four on the afternoon of a hot August 30th, 1962. Three weeks earlier, my fiancé had pinned Air Force pilot's wings on my chest at Williams Field, Arizona. As a next assignment, I chose the C-130E Hercules transport, a brand-new model just coming off the Lockheed Aircraft assembly lines, so eight weeks of C-130 training at Sewart lay ahead.

I had never seen a C-130 up close. Coming across the country, I'd spotted one far away in the air, recognizable by its distinctive high tailfin and the deep, throaty rumble of its engines. I knew it only by reputation: Powerful, reliable, and able to land and take off from anywhere. Short runways, grass strips, remote areas. Equipped with skis, they even flew it onto the Antarctic ice pack to resupply Little America.

I signed in at the base HQ, got my BOQ assignment, then hustled in the gathering dusk toward the flight line, anxious to have a first look at the bird.

The airfield was quiet now, training operations done for the day. I came around the corner of an enormous hangar and there it was. Or rather, there they were. Arrayed in neat lines stretching into the graying distance was an entire squadron of Herky-birds.

I approached the nearest aircraft, trying to absorb what I was seeing. As a new pilot fresh from training in small fighter-type planes, I was staggered by the size of it. Four massive jet engines hung along the leading edge of a high wing that stretched nearly half a football field. Each engine was fronted with an immense paddle-blade propeller so large it looked like it belonged on a Dutch windmill.

Under that big wing, the huge round belly of the craft squatted low to the ground to allow easy loading of troops, cargo and equipment. Four of the biggest, fattest tires I had ever seen emerged from pods on each side of the fuselage. Two to a side, arranged in tandem, they were almost as high as I was. They would support heavy-laden planes landing on primitive dirt fields near the front lines.

Impressed as I was with its mass and utilitarian design, I saw that this was far from a pretty airplane. At the front of the fuselage below the cockpit was a big, black, bulbous clown nose of a radar dome. For a moment, I imagined this plane, its nose painted bright red, leading Santa's way on a stormy Christmas Eve.

I continued my gawking walk beneath one of the long, cylindrical fuel tanks suspended under the wing between the engines, and I felt like Dopey, the dwarf. Could I ever manage this thing? On the ground, even, let alone in the air. How could I ever taxi this behemoth without running it into something? Would I ever get this ungainly beast airborne? Fly it? And how the hell was I going to get it back on the ground? I tried to tamp down my anxieties. Plenty of pilots had done it before me. That's what I was here for—to learn how to do all that.

It was getting dark. I went back to the BOQ, realizing that soon I would be expected to pilot this monster. I didn't sleep well that night.

***

We reported to Flight Operations at 0500 next morning—"O-Dark-Hundred" in Air Force parlance—for our orientation flight. There, my roommate for the duration, Gary Knutsen, a stocky blonde kid from Minnesota, and I met our instructor, Major Bob Byers.

Laid-back Major Bob looked every bit the old pilot. Command pilot wings adorned his rumpled gray-green flight suit. A "fifty-mission crush" hat with "scrambled eggs" on its bill sat cocked on his head, poorly concealing a not so closely-cropped head of graying dark hair. A short, well-chewed old stogie, unlit, jutted (at five in the morning!) from beneath the luxuriant handlebar mustache. It added to the mystique, but could not hide the lazy grin. Crow's feet spread from the corners of his twinkling eyes. This, and the prairie wind complexion made us feel that, when it came to flying, Major Bob had been there and done that.

"Boys, this airplane's a pussycat to fly, but when you're in that left seat, you'll have a tiger by the tail. She'll do whatever you ask her to within reason, but you jet jockeys need to learn what reason's boundaries are. Let's go aviate. Willard, I'm gonna put you in the left seat first. Knutsen can watch and learn from your mistakes."

"Er, um, Major, I only just saw this airplane for the first time last night. I'll have no idea what I'm doing."

"That's what I'm here for lieutenant, to save us from yourself. You're gonna learn by doing. School of hard landings, and all that. Grab your gear and let's check the weather. Then we'll go out and introduce you to the Herk by way of the preflight."

The preflight is the visual inspection of the airplane by an outside walk-around, then, in the C-130's case, the inside too. We did the outside, then climbed the foldout steps into the belly of the bird. The cavernous cargo bay, long as a bowling alley and wide as two of them, extended away from where we stood, backward toward the closed full-width loading ramp at the tail end. I could envision tanks and six-bys crawling up that ramp.

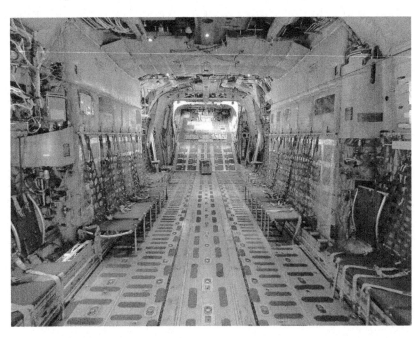

Bundles of cables, wires and tubes ran the length of the compartment and crammed every space around the periphery of the interior. Acoustic padding lined the few areas where the cable and wires weren't, but its existence was negated by the howl of the gas turbine aux power unit and the high-pitched, 400-cycle whine of a bevy of exposed motors, already set running by the flight engineer. It was loud in here now, even without the engines running. I wondered what this big echo chamber would sound like when we fired up those four roaring jets with their big whirling props.

Canvas seats with webbed backrests, each with its own seatbelt, were set up along the sides.

"Those are for the paratroops. When we finish our flight, this aircraft is scheduled to run down to Pope and practice dropping troops this afternoon." This from Major Bob. "You'll be doing that yourselves in a few weeks."

Pope AFB was next to Fort Bragg in North Carolina, the Army's paratroop school. Practicing to drop troops meant practicing for combat situations.

Major Bob continued, "Combat drop in a C-130: Go 'balls to the wall' as fast and low as you can over the enemy terrain, then pop up to jump altitude, 1,000 feet, slow her down to 125 knots, and open the doors. Low, slow and unarmed. Pucker time. Icy trickle down the spine. You never saw a bunch of guys so glad to jump out of an airplane. They barely have time to get their helmets back on their heads after they've puked their guts out into them."

Knutsen looked at me and I looked back. Harsh reality was beginning to set in. Major Bob's slow grin got a bit wider.

We continued our preflight, climbing a few steps to the flight deck. The area was huge. We could actually walk around up here.

C-130 cockpit

The two pilots sat side by side up front, looking out on their surroundings through large panels of NESA glass. Much better visibility than most other multi-engine aircraft. No wonder they called this the greenhouse. I could see everywhere except to the rear. This made me nervous until Major Bob explained that I could check the radar for any bogies. Bogies on my tail in a C-130—that thought made me more nervous. And later, I found out the radar only looked forward.

The pilots had a broad console between them that held the throttles, engine condition levers, flap handle, auto pilot controls and an array of radio gear. Just behind this console sat the flight engineer. He managed the aircraft systems—electrical, hydraulic, fuel, engine controls, HVAC—from an immense, complicated panel that spread across the ceiling of the cockpit.

To the right rear of the flight engineer was the navigator's station, with a large desk where he could lay out his maps and plot the course. Over this work surface was his own complex panel of gages and navigational electronics—radar, doppler radar, LORAN. There was also a place to store the sextant, an optical device the navigator poked through the ceiling of the aircraft like a periscope. He used it to sight specific stars and calculate our position from his readings. No GPS in those days.

At the left rear of the flight deck was a galley with a small electric oven for heating food, and a three-gallon plug-in coffee pot. I imagined what that *joe* would taste like after a long flight—that is, if it wasn't too thick to pour.

To my amazement, the C-130 had a couple of bunks, one above the other on the back wall of the flight deck. These were spacious and easy to access, better than the ones in an old railroad Pullman car. With crew duty days up to 30 hours long, it was important for those off duty to have a place to rest. I found out later that rest did not come easily. Noise from the engines was so loud it was exhausting. It seemed the more I slept, the "tireder" I got.

The next big surprise was that, for a C-130, the walk-around inspection included walking around on top of the aircraft. A hatch in the ceiling over the upper bunk accessed the roof of the fuselage. Up I went, scrambling onto the top of the airplane. Nice view from up here.

I walked back to where the wings crossed the body and out onto each, inspecting engines and props, fuel access points, ailerons and flaps and the life raft compartments near the trailing edge of each wing. Four twenty-man life rafts, compressed into folded wads, were stored there. I returned to the fuselage and walked back to toward the tail. The vertical stabilizer towered above me, and the horizontal tail surfaces spread out in both directions, larger by far than the wings of the T-33 I had just finished flying in pilot training.

Done up top, I wriggled back down the hatch into the cockpit. Preflight was finished and we were ready to go. I took my place in the left seat. The morning was cool, but the back of my flight suit was soaked with sweat. Turns out, my trepidations were groundless. Major Bob was a superbly competent and laid-back instructor, not an up-tight ass-chewer like some of my pilot training IP's. Taxiing was actually easy. I just sat myself over the white line on the tarmac and followed it to the runway. There was even a little steering wheel to use for taxiing. No more cocked nose gear.

Out at the end of the runway, I set the brakes and pushed the throttles to takeoff power. The C-130's engines run at the same speed all the time. Pushing the throttles increases the pitch of the props and they chew more air. Pull back to idle, and the prop pitch flattens. Then they have no bite. It's like having four big barn doors out there impeding your progress. Slows you down in a hurry.

But "balls to the wall" with the brakes locked, the throaty roar is at its max. She shudders and vibrates, trembling with anxiety, like a bulldog on a leash wanting to get at an alley cat. Release the brakes and back into the seat you go. The roll gathers rapidly. Before you know it, it's time to rotate and fly.

The flying itself was pretty easy. Learning all the airplane's systems within the eight weeks was the challenging part. The operations manual—the aircraft's "Bible"—was as big and thick as an old family Bible. The pilot had to know that book cold. Lots of late nights during those eight weeks.

***

Just past the middle of October, two weeks before the end of school, we got a wake-up call—in more ways than one. Around 0100 hours, some SOB pounding on our BOQ door awakened Gary Knutsen and me from a sound sleep.

"Wake up! It's Major Byers. We've been alerted."

"Go to hell, Swanson, you drunken bum. We know it's you."

"This is Byers. Get your sorry asses out here in five minutes or I'll have the AP's bust this door down."

The grogginess was leaving fast. Was this the laid-back Major Bob threatening to break down our door? Couldn't be. Fully alert now, we erred on the side of caution and opened up. It was Major Byers.

"We've been alerted. We've got to fly to New Mexico and bring some fighter squadron equipment back to Homestead in Florida."

"What's the big deal? Why the middle of the night?"

"Did you hear Kennedy's speech to the nation last night?"

"No. We were studying for tomorrow's test."

"Well, tomorrow's test has been scrubbed. The Russians have got missiles in Cuba and it looks like there's gonna be one hell of a war. This equipment belongs to a New Mexico F-100 squadron that's gonna' stage out of Homestead. When we get to Homestead, so are we. If the excrement hits the prop, we're gonna drop troops into 'Cuber'." Byers said, using Kennedy's accent.

"Helig Skit!" From Knutsen.

"What?"

"That's Swedish for 'holy shit'."

My Air Force career had begun in earnest. Looked like it wasn't going to be four years of passenger runs and freight hauls after all.

Overheat!

Charles F. Willard

An inky black night, 28,000 feet over the western Pacific. Seven hours into a flight from the Midway Islands, inbound to Kadena Air Base, Okinawa. So far, the journey across nearly 7,000 miles of ocean is uneventful, but, for a green pilot with less than 100 hours in the C-130 aircraft, it is not the boring slog that it would become in a few years. There is too much to learn.

Instrument lights set at their dimmest, autopilot flying the aircraft, I sit in the left seat with my feet propped on the rests at the base of the instrument panel, the static of the HF radio crackling in my headset. The flight engineer, Staff Sergeant Lou Barbieri, in his seat off my right shoulder, and I are the only crewmembers awake to monitor the gauges and make sure everything stays on an even keel. The navigator, Lieutenant Al Boettger is resting at his station, head in his arms on the chart table. The other two pilots, the aircraft commander, Captain Dick Davis, and the first pilot, Lieutenant Gordon Almquist, are fast asleep in the crew bunks, one over the other, at the rear bulkhead of the flight deck.

WONK! WONK! WONK! WONK!

With no warning, earsplitting blasts come from the emergency claxon and reverberate through the cockpit, overwhelming the throaty roar of the four turboprop engines. Intense crimson flashes, synchronized to the *WONK–WONK*s, pulse lightning-like from one of the engine shut-down T-handles that jut from the panel above my head, filling the flight deck with eerie, throbbing red light.

The sudden auditory and visual violence startles me and sends an instant convulsion of panic up my spine.

"Overheat indication on number two engine." The calm voice of Sgt. Barbieri. In his several thousand hours in this bird, he has evidently seen this kind of thing before.

"Feather number two." I hear myself reply, my shaky voice echoing into my own earphones. Training has kicked in.

Sgt. Barbieri reaches forward and pulls the offending T-handle. Immediately the raucous clamor and blinding dazzle cease and I can hear the rapid wind-down of the engine. Craning my neck to the left, I look out at the wing in time to see the number two prop slow and come to a stop, its four paddles standing at silent attention, 90 degrees to the slipstream. There is no visible sign of fire.

"Emergency shutdown checklist." Me again. Training again.

"What the hell just happened?" It is Captain Davis this time, rudely awakened from his snoring in the upper bunk. His wide eyes look like two pee-holes in his unshaven face.

"Overheat on number two. We're running the shut-down checklist now."

"All right. Move your ass over to the right seat, Willard, and let me in there."

He slides into the left seat where I had been, and buckles up. "I've got the aircraft," he says. We run the checklist. "OK, Willard, what do we do now?"

"I contact Kadena Approach and declare an emergency."

"Right you are. Do it." I check the Kadena frequency and key the mike:

"Kadena Approach, MATS 21788."

"MATS 21788, Kadena. Good morning."

"Kadena, 788. Good morning. 788 is a C-130E inbound to Kadena. We've had to shut down our number two engine. We are declaring an emergency at this time." This is standard procedure any time a MATS (Military Air Transport Service) aircraft loses an engine. While a C-130 has no problem flying on three engines, trouble might come later if a second engine has to be shut down.

"Roger, 788. We will have emergency crews standing by. What is your position and ETA, Kadena?"

"Chuck, we're estimating Kadena at 1412 Zulu." This from Al Boettger on the intercom. A little excitement in the cockpit gets everyone instantly on the job.

"Kadena, 788. We're estimating your station at 1412 Zulu. We're leaving 28,000 feet for 24,000. We can hold that altitude on three engines." This from Captain Davis.

"Roger, 788."

In a moment, "Mats 21788, Kadena. You're about two hours out. Would you like an escort?"

"No need, Kadena. We'll do fine on three engines. 788."

"Um, 788, Kadena. We, ahh, have an Air-Sea Rescue Squadron here, and they'd, ahh, like a little practice. Would you mind if we scrambled an SA-16?"

A chuckle from Captain Davis before he keys the mike. "Ok. I understand. Go ahead. We'll be looking for him after a while."

"Thank you, 788. Kadena out."

The chuckling from Davis turns into downright laughter. "I don't understand, Sir. What's so funny?"

"Willard, Are you at all familiar with the SA-16 Albatross aircraft?"

"No, Sir."

"Well, it's like this. We're two hours out, making 300 knots. It'll take those guys about 30 minutes to get in the air. An SA-16 cruises at 108 knots. By the time they intercept us, we'll be on final approach to Kadena. But we'll let them have their practice."

Sure enough, we are about thirty miles out of Kadena when we spot the SA-16 below, churning along toward us at a snail's pace. We have to throttle way back and mush through the air so we don't outrun him. Hanging on our three remaining props, we let him escort us down final approach to an uneventful landing—except for all the crash trucks following us down the runway, and a wing-waggle from the Albatross as he motors slowly by overhead.

We are thankful for the careful attention. Those Air-Sea Rescue guys can be the difference between life and death when you need them.

By the way, the cause of the overheat indication is a faulty sensor. A couple hours to replace it, refuel and eat breakfast, and we are on our way to 'Nam.

The Congo Caper

Charles F. Willard

Throughout its history, the Congo has often been violent and unstable. It was particularly so during the last months of 1964, when, during a period of rebellion and tribal warfare, more than 150 missionaries were abducted, tortured and killed.

Survivors were few, and they told harrowing stories of their experiences. The United Stated Air Force, while not involved in their direct rescue, flew many of the survivors on C-130 aircraft from the areas of unrest to the temporarily safe haven of Leopoldville.

Like many areas of the world during the Cold War, the Congo, rich in resources and strategically located, became a geopolitical battleground between the USSR, the Chinese and their proxies, and the United States and its allies. The area seemed a-boil with volatility. It was rumored that the Chinese had an estimated 20,000 troops and advisors stationed just across the river from Leopoldville, waiting for the right moment to invade.

During the last days of 1964, I found myself assigned as one of the pilots on an Air Force C-130 mission from Charleston Air Force Base, South Carolina into this area.

***

Our aircrew is alerted early on the morning after Christmas. Arriving at Base Ops we get our flight orders and read them through. It looks like it is going to be a strange and different mission. Leopoldville, Congo is to be our turnaround destination, but we will have plenty of work to do before we get that far.

This is the "beat the Russians to the moon" decade. Launches of missiles from Cape Canaveral are a regular happening, both for the Gemini program of the space race, and for other, more clandestine military activities. Each of these launches requires tracking, so our country has technical personnel "marooned" on many remote outposts scattered along the paths the missiles take, down across the Caribbean, over eastern South America and out to the vastness of the South Atlantic, toward Africa and beyond.

As we study our manifests, they reveal a curious mix of freight, and one passenger. There are pallets of supplies for our missile tracking stations—everything from toilet paper and belated Christmas presents for those poor, lonely souls manning the telemetry, to replacement electronic parts for their gear. A separate pallet holds a resupply of body bags for Leopoldville. The chaos in the Congo is unabated.

Our lone passenger is the base chaplain.

He brings along his own cargo: Two cases of communion wine. As we stop at each tracking station, he has his own mission: Offer a belated Christmas communion for any of those isolated personnel so inclined.

We get the wheels in the well on schedule and by 0900 we are on the ground at Grand Bahama Island, offloading the GBI pallet. We delay our takeoff long enough for the Padre to do his job, then we island-hop to the next stops, Eleuthra, then San Salvador. Landing on tiny San Salvador is always "interesting." The (very short) runway begins at the seashore on one side, humpbacks over the narrow island to the other

Vietnam

side, where the end of it disappears into the ocean at high tide. No long, hot landings here or we'll all be swimming.

Staying dry on San Sal, we go on to Aruba, then Georgetown, British Guiana, Paramaribo in Surinam and down across the equator into Recife on the east coast of Brazil where, after 30 hours of "gear up, gear down," we rest.

Our flight resumes the next day and we head out across the 3,500-mile-wide South Atlantic. Dead reckoning now, no more line-of-sight radio beacons till we get to Ascension Island, a volcanic dot over 1,400 miles away. There's nothing else out here. If we have a problem, we're fish food. Props, keep a churnin'. Navigator, do your stuff.

Our "navi-guesser" finds the dot, we refuel our plane while the Padre is busy refueling his flock, then we are off into the night, headed to Leopoldville, our turn-around point over 2,000 miles away. That's about seven hours flying time in a C-130. Africa is a lot bigger than Ascension, so no sweat finding it, and the aircraft has run flawlessly the whole way. We have been "losing time" as we fly steadily east. Leopoldville is about six time zones ahead of Charleston. We are on the ground there by about noon, Congo time.

Because of the unrest in the region, our orders are to discharge our cargo—the body bags and the gear for the tracking personnel—refuel and get the heck out of here as fast as we can, back to Ascension.

So far so good. Fred Vogel is the designated aircraft commander for this flight. He's in the left seat and I'm in the right seat, copilot for this leg. By 1530 (3:30 p.m. to you civilians), I am running the "start engines" checklist. With the time difference, we'll be back at Ascension in time to hit the "O" club.

"Start number three."

"Starting three." Vogel pushes in the #3 start button and holds it there, waiting for the RPM to hit 30%.

I crane my neck around to the right and watch as the number three prop begins to spool up. "Three's spinning…oh shit! Three just blew a seal and there's prop oil all over the ramp. Shut down three."

The collective groan from everyone seems to make the sides of the aircraft bulge out.

"What are we gonna' do now?"

"We could try a three-engine takeoff."

"No, that's only authorized in time of war. The situation here is volatile, but it ain't war yet. We'd get our asses in a sling if we tried it."

"That means we're stuck here. We can't even get a hold of Charleston to let them know our situation."

"We got one faint hope. If we can get Charleston on the HF, we can ask them to send us a prop."

HF radios work by bouncing their signals off the ionosphere. They do fairly well when an aircraft is in the air at night, but in the daytime, on the ground to a station 7,000 miles away, it is, shall we say, "iffy."

"Say a prayer, Padre." Vogel keys the HF:

"Charleston, this is MATS 21792." We *all* say a prayer.

"MATS 21792, Charleston. Go ahead." Wow! Nothing like the power of prayer.

"Charleston, 21792 is on the ground at Ndjili Airport, Leopoldville. We've lost a prop. Can you send us a replacement?" There is a delay. The thought goes through everyone's mind: *Have we lost radio contact?* After a long, tense moment,

"792, Charleston. Roger on the prop. We can have it on a C-130 in the morning. It should be there in three or four days. Charleston out."

Another collective exhale. Was it a sigh of relief or a groan? Three or four days in the Congo? Gulp.

They tow our busted airplane into a humongous hanger and park it next to the pallet of body bags we just unloaded. Gad! If all the rumors are true, it could be *our* bodies going home in those bags.

Up the stairs to what passes for Base Ops. We notice what look like bullet holes in the woodwork and pock marks in the concrete. We inquire. Yes, they are bullet holes. "There was a recent skirmish," the Congolese Ops officer says, casually. Shaken, but trying not to show it, we ask about lodging. No quarters are available. It is the "Lockheed Hotel" for the duration.

Supper is a foul-tasting hamburger from the greasy-grungy airport canteen. (What'll it be, bullets or ptomaine?) Nursing heartburn, we straggle back to the aircraft to see what we have for bedding to soften the floor of the now-empty cargo bay. Suddenly we realize it is New Year's Eve.

Throughout the trying afternoon, the base chaplain, the oldest of us by a couple of decades, has been a calming influence on this young crew (we are all in our twenties). Now he comes to the rescue again.

"Cheer up, men, I still have half a case of communion wine."

We welcome in the New Year sitting on the cargo floor of the "Lockheed Hotel," playing poker for matchsticks and drinking the rest of the communion wine. We bed down, now without a care in the world, and drift into dreamland on the aluminum mattress.

The waking comes rude and sudden at about three a.m. Gunfire. Heavy machineguns, and not too far away. Our airplane is dark and buttoned up. That—and cower in the dark—is all we can do. Dawn comes and the noise stops. All is calm for a while and we timidly make our way up to Base Ops to get the story.

"We got defensive machinegun placements surrounding the airport. One of them heard a suspicious noise and started shooting. Another thought he was being fired on and shot back, until it was light enough to see what was going on. Nobody hurt."

Was that a blessing or a curse? Protected from invaders by the world's worst marksmen.

***

We are stuck here for three more days. No more gunfire. Maybe they used all their ammo. About noon the third day we see a C-130 on final approach. It is our rescue airplane. They have our prop. Yippee!

The story is not over yet. We pull rank. The rule is that the aircrew who has been out the longest can commandeer the aircraft of any crew who has been out less long. So, when our rescuers' airplane is refueled, we take it and wave goodbye to them and to the Congo. No good deed goes unpunished.

The story is not over yet. We land at Ascension and spend a relaxing evening at the club and a peaceful night resting at the comfortable Royal Air Force BOQ (Ascension is a British possession). In the morning, we preflight our aircraft and find the generator on number four engine is inoperative. Of course, no parts are available; they will have to be flown in from Charleston. Just as we are cursing our luck, here comes good old 21792 down final, prop all repaired. Guess what? We take our rescuers' aircraft again and fly home. No good deed goes unpunished, II.

Good old 21792 landing on Ascension Island

Air Crash

Charles F. Willard

The alert came at 0500 for an 0600 preflight. I tiptoed down the open steel steps from our second-floor flat, trying not to wake Mrs. Meservy, our landlady, who resided on the first floor of the single-house in downtown Charleston, South Carolina. An indolent, damp breeze was moseying in from the sea, its wetness spawning a low, drifting fog that intensified as it passed over the ever-oozing chimney stacks of the pulp and paper mill in North Charleston. It looked a pale yellow-green in the headlights, a typical Charleston spring morning pea soup ground fog, and it slowed the predawn traffic on the "dual lane" to a crawl. By the time I stepped from the car at Base Ops, the murk was thick as gruel and I could feel its sogginess on my face. "Zero-zero and the birds are walking" was the proper meteorological term for it.

But we went ahead with our C-130 flight preparations. The fog would burn off when the sun rose far enough out of the sea. At the aircraft, using flashlights, we did the walk-around, outside and in, then climbed the crew ladder to the flight deck. Popping the top hatch, I scrambled up onto the roof of the aircraft—into a bright, slanting sun! The fog, still lingering unperturbed below, and fragrant with the sulfurous paper mill odor, was only about 15 feet thick, wisps of it wafting about my boots as I made my careful way over the tops of the wings and fuselage. It was a strange sight. A vast white meadow with only tail fins, tops of hangars and the control tower sprouting from it, like shark fins and giant bread loaves and a church steeple poking out of a snowfield.

By the time we were ready to start engines, the sun had worked its magic and the fog made its retreat. The weather was CAVU (Ceiling and Visibility Unlimited) now, but the forecast for our first stop, Naval Air Station Norfolk, was iffy—squalls and thundershowers.

An hour and a half later, we landed there between the gusts and raindrops. Leaving our two loadmasters to oversee the cargo operations, the rest of us took the crew bus around the end of the runway to Base Ops. We spent the next couple of hours flight-planning the subsequent legs of our mission, first to Lajes in the Azores off the coast of Portugal for refueling, then on to Rota, Spain, near Gibraltar for crew rest before going on to several stops in Africa. After a bite of lunch at the cafeteria, it was time to get back to the aircraft. The weather was still squally, with low rainclouds sweeping over the field, and an occasional lightning bolt zinging to the ground in the distance. Our drive on the perimeter road back to the plane was halted short of the runway overrun by a radio call from the tower. A Navy P2V Neptune was on final approach after a long overnight flight.

The Lockheed P2V was a good-sized twin engine aircraft. Designed during the latter part of World War II, it was, until the mid-sixties, the Navy's primary anti-submarine hunter. It was full of electronic gear—a belly-mounted surface search radar that could detect subs at long distances, a "magnetic anomaly detector" to track submerged "bogies," and a bunch of sonar buoys that could be dropped over enemy targets, enabling destroyers to move in for the kill.

During those years, when the cold war was at its peak, the Navy had these planes in the air off the US east coast around the clock, keeping their electronic eyes and ears peeled for Soviet submarines. The Neptune carried a crew of ten, most of whom manned the electronics.

From our vantage point off the end of the runway, we watched the Neptune, gear and flaps down, descending like an awkward seabird, pitching and yawing in the gusting wind. The final approach to landing is when an aircraft is at its most vulnerable. All its high-drag components (landing gear, flaps, speed brakes, etc.) are deployed. Its speed and altitude are low and decreasing. The engines are at minimum power. It has little chance to recover from mechanical failure or human miscalculation—or a weather anomaly.

We could barely see it coming through the heavy, scudding clouds and pelting rain. Then, when it was about 50 feet in the air, just above the overrun, we lost sight of it. The plane, not 500 feet from us, had disappeared into the roiling murk of an onrushing squall. A collective shiver went through us. We knew the pilot, at this most critical point of the landing, could no longer see the runway.

When the plane next appeared to us, it was falling out of the air. It pancaked onto the end of the airstrip, the descent so hard that the right landing gear was driven through the wing. We gaped, unbelieving, petrified by what we were seeing. The right wing separated, and, as the remainder of the craft cartwheeled down the runway, the spewing gasoline exploded and engulfed the spinning airframe in a blinding hundred-foot-high inferno.

The Neptune came to rest in the grass about a thousand feet away. The flames, unabated, grew even higher. We watched helpless and in horror, sick at our stomachs. We had just seen ten fellow servicemen meet a sudden and awful death. At that time, we were still a young crew. None of us had yet been exposed to the harsh and violent finality of an air crash, and it shook us to our cores.

What happened next was hard to comprehend because of its suddenness. Several big yellow crash trucks appeared as if someone had snapped their fingers. Each had massive twin fire nozzles mounted to the tops of their cabs. From these cannons spewed tsunamis of foam that pushed the wall of flames away from the port side of the aircraft. Momentarily, small figures began to emerge from the fuselage. We counted. One. Two. There's three, four, five. Six. Seven, eight. Then, from the broken tail section, came nine and ten, one helping the other stumble away from the flames. They all had escaped!

Our gut-wrenching horror turned to an awed and shaky relief. It took two hours to clear the debris and reopen the field. Two hours to calm our shaken souls and celebrate the saving of ten others.

We had to go fly then.

"Waterboarding," Air Force Style

Charles F. Willard

Many regard waterboarding as torture. Water is poured into the mouth of a restrained prisoner until he begins to choke, and he is allowed to think he will drown.

Back in the early Sixties, we new Air Force pilots were required to complete a rigorous three weeks of survival training. As a part of that program, we found ourselves in circumstances like those of a restrained and waterboarded prisoner.

It was not a simulated torture. Rather, it was training on how to survive a ditching at sea. The Air Force wanted us to experience what could happen if we had to set our aircraft down in the water. Knowing beforehand the way it might go, and what to do about it, could help us live through an otherwise unsurvivable situation.

We are not all as skilled and fortunate as Captain Sully Sullenberger, who some years ago, successfully ditched his Air Bus 320 in the Hudson River and saved all 155 passengers and crew. Trying to survive a ditching in a wind-blown, choppy ocean might be just a bit *dicier*.

Most times, statistically, a ditching is less than successful. Often, the nose of the aircraft catches a wave, somersaulting the plane onto its back, submerging the cockpit. The pilot, if he has survived the flipping, is left trapped underwater, upside down, hanging from his shoulder straps.

Here is how the USAF ditching training went, to the best of my recollection:

There is a big, deep, Olympic-sized pool. Suspended over it on hydraulic arms is the cockpit of a fighter jet. I am in full flying gear—flight suit and flying boots, helmet and oxygen mask, seat-pack parachute banging against the backs of my thighs as I am led up the gangplank to the cockpit. The canopy is missing. It would have been jettisoned before impact with the water. I climb into the cramped space and settle onto the seat. The sergeant escorting me leans over and helps me buckle in. Parachute straps cinched tight. Likewise, seat belt and shoulder harness, secured by a single clasp at my waist. Oxygen hose and radio cables plugged into their receptacles. Helmet visor down, oxygen mask clamped to my face.

"Are you ready, lieutenant?"

I have one hand on the stick, the other on the throttle, feet on the rudder pedals, just as instructed. My knees are shaking. I give a nod to the sergeant. He descends the gangplank and pulls it away. I wait. An eternal moment goes by.

With a suddenness I was dreading, the hydraulic mechanism releases, flipping the cockpit and plunging it into the pool. I am slammed against the straps. The violence of the maneuver is disorienting, and pain wracks my shoulders as the straps dig in. Did I remember to take a breath? Too late now. The water roils around me. Panic stabs at me like a hundred knives. My mind races. Can I remember the sequence from my training? If I get it wrong, I'll get all fouled up and won't be able to get out before I breathe in water.

Release the radio cable and oxygen mask. (There goes my lifeline—no good to me underwater). Now the helmet. Fumble to unstrap it, wrench it off, push it away. Lungs are burning now. The seat belt and shoulder harness. Where is that latch? Precious seconds gone. Shaky fingers grope and find it. Quivering with anxiety now, lungs on fire. Whole body shaking from fear and cold. Brain, stay focused. Next, the damned parachute buckles. Unstrap! Unstrap! Fingers don't work. There. Finally. Struggle out of the chute. Kick down. Foot on the canopy rail. Push with the leaden, soggy boots. Flail upward against the weight. Lungs are done. Head clears the surface. Gasping breath of freedom for the aching, bursting lungs. Frogman on each side of me now, supporting me in the water, guiding me to pool's edge. I never saw them down there. They would have pulled me out if they had to.

If they'd pulled me out, I would have had to do it all again—until I got it right or quit. If I had failed, no more pilot for me. I would be off to navigator school. Could have easily gone that way, but it didn't. Waterboarding, Air Force style.

Cheating Death

Charles F. Willard

Since you are still around to read this at whatever your ripe old age is, I suspect you can think of several times when you have "cheated death." My own experiences with this phenomenon began early and have continued with an alarming frequency throughout a thankfully long life.

They began on a family vacation when I was a 20-month-old. Dad was a few yards out from shore, trying to teach Mom to swim. I was building sand castles on the beach in the care of Mary, my teen-age baby sitter. She glanced at me once in a while as she paged through her Hollywood fan magazine.

Sand castles got boring. I saw Mom and Dad out there in the water having fun. It didn't take long to for me to escape Mary's attention and wade out toward Mom and Dad. In a few steps, I was up to my neck in the ocean, water lapping at my mouth, toes barely touching bottom. Fortune would have it that Mom spotted me before I was swept off my feet and into eternal oblivion. My first time cheating death.

Like many of us, I had several more of these "dumb kid" experiences growing up. You would think that, once into adulthood, "cheating death" incidents would abate. *Au contraire.* Enter the US Air Force. First, pilot training had its moments. I've already related the hypoxia episode in the T-37 and the near mid-air collision in the T-33. I cheated death, but six months later, three of my four Pilot Training instructors had died in air crashes.

And my near-death experiences in 2,000 hours of flying the C-130, that safe, sedate, subsonic, multi-engine, non-combat (hah!) Air Force transport are legion but not legendary. That's what comes of flying all kinds of missions all over the world including combat zones and to remote, unprepared airfields, in all kinds of weather and over all manner of terrain with little to guide you to the ground but sharp eyes, quick reflexes and the seat of your pants.

That's what the C-130 is designed to do, but still…. It seems that 15% of all the C-130's ever built—and they've been building them for over 60 years, now—have met a violent end.

"Cheated death again." That's what you say to your crew chief as you step wearily down from the cockpit back onto Mother Earth after a particularly hairy mission, and it is likely to be accompanied by a relieved grin and a shaky hand moving across a sweat-soaked forehead.

Thankfully, for me, those days are long past. Still, as the old Hank Williams song affirms, "I'll never get out of this world alive."

Boots in the Air

Charles F. Willard

When we hear the phrase "boots on the ground," right away we think about the need to put our fighting men into harm's way on the ground in enemy territory.

But airmen wear boots too, for several good reasons.

First, most air missions are flown at high altitudes where outside temperatures are way below zero. In most military planes the only things between those temperatures and the airman's feet are the thin aluminum skin of the aircraft and a pair of heavy flying boots with a couple of pairs of insulated socks.

Second, the heavy shanks and high tops of those properly laced boots protect feet and ankles from fracture in a rough parachute landing. And, "those boots are made for walking." They are your foot and leg armor when the only path to evasion and survival is through tangled underbrush and over rugged terrain.

Finally, those boots are protection for the airman's feet, even in death. The Air Force "footprints" all its airmen. The footprints are kept on file. Often the only thing left in the ashy wreckage of an air crash is the charred remains of a boot, holding a still-intact foot, identifiable by those footprints.

Angel of Death or Peace

Gary T. Redlinski

How many times must a veteran die before he finds peace? I died this year on Veterans Day.

I died in Vietnam, death was all around me, so many years ago.

A vet friend once asked me why I relive it every year. For him it may be simple, but I live it every day. I lived and worked with death every day for two years. It was my job.

I died in Nam, I just didn't know it. People and family said I was different when I came home. I fought my way back 'til I hit my wall.

I died again.

I fought my way back, again.

I hit my wall again, when I realized that suicide kid, with no head, flashed me back to Nam.

I died again.

There were thousands of remains (that's all they were) that passed through my hands.

I don't know where their spirits went, but I know their bodies went thru hell.

I died again.

I think of them daily, and I die each time.

My spirit is gone... my body's still here.

I hope to arise by Memorial Day (which now sounds like a long time from now), in time to die again.

"Two years were two days, too long"

Gary T. Redlinski

You've always been with me since those two fateful years. Its 24 years now. You'll probably stay with me for the next 24—if I make it that far. If there's a heaven or a hell, maybe we'll meet again. When we first met—you were bloody and dirty, sometimes bloated and green, some charred to no end: sometimes whole, sometimes not. I pieced you together as best as I could. The maggots were gross and the smell sometimes unbearable. I put your bone fragments together; it was like working on a jigsaw puzzle. So we could give you a name.

We were so young—both you and I. If only I'd known two years would be too much.

What do I see when the flashbacks occur? It's usually you lying on that porcelain table, burnt to a crisp.

I used a power bone cutter to cut through your jaw, to be able to look at your teeth.

God, you were ugly and messy with your dried or oozing blood all over everything, your clothes, sometimes on mine. You had blown out holes in your body, and your guts would hang out. Too many times your brains weren't in your head. I never got used to that smell—it always made me gag. To this day I'm leery of that smell.

There were times when I broke your fingers or arms trying to "break" the rigor that set in.

The fingers were clenched in a fist, either from rigor, or when burnt in a fire. Sometimes as a "floater," I put your layer of skin over my hand, it felt like a glove. I did anything I could to get a good fingerprint so we could identify you and send you home to your family. I couldn't afford to make mistakes. You had to be you—to give you a name.

I remember when four or five of you came in from a chopper crash. You also came with a burlap bag. The bag was filled with your parts—an arm or two, a leg and a head, with only a scratch or two on your cheek—but not attached to the rest of you. When we put you together, your head belonged to the worst of you which was badly burnt to a crisp.

Sometimes you were only a lump of flesh. Sometimes you were sort of flat or blown all apart. Hopefully most of you went fast. I know a lot of you didn't.

I remember you that looked like boiled sausage, puffy, gray, no skin left, all sliced along your arms and legs to prevent you from bursting, while you still lived. You were so slippery from being covered with cream to keep from drying. You were awful to handle, hard to get prints from.

Did I mention the maggots you brought me? White squirmy things, wiggling all over.... Sometimes they were all over you, crawling out of your wounds, your nose, and your mouth. They were so hard to kill. We poured chloroform in your green body bag, it didn't always kill them, but at least it slowed them down. It probably killed you though, in case you weren't. Just another of your damn gross accounts.

I remember the C-130 we unloaded, where one of (30 or so) decided to leak out of your bag and all over the plane. You were a floater and you must have broke—green and brown ooze with such stench that made everyone gag.

Is this why I'm angry? Is this why I'm sad? Is this why I hurt so much? I cry and I cry but it always comes back. Why did you take so long to come back?

You were young, some of you not so young, you were kids, you were men. Some of you I never saw. Some of you were just reports, coordinates and places listed on maps, you were missing. Some of you were listed in places where our Government said we weren't. So I just gave you, "*coordinates unknown.*"

We had a joke at the mortuary, "22 tables—no waiting," but sometimes you came so fast and in such bunches, that you just lie there and wait for a space.

The government knew it wouldn't be short. That's why they built such a new complex, just waiting for you. It had coolers the size of rooms. One was a waiting room. The others were places to stay until you could be embalmed, then sent back to your folks.

Sometimes we put you on racks on the walls. When it was busy, you were stacked in the middle of the floors.

God, how you stunk, how ugly you were. Getting used to you day by day was a bitch.

I guess I never really grieved for you then. After all, we never made friends. Now, since the Gulf War, I hurt so damn bad. I don't know why. Maybe because, you don't "KILL" buildings or tanks, You "KILL" *people* who are in those things.

Now that I'm here at the "WALL," I first cried and I cried, but that has gone past (at least for now). There are so many who pass by your names. Most of them have no idea of what it was like. None of them, not even me, know what you went through, for if they did, they'd be up on the Wall just like you.

How can I imagine what you went through—you lived in mud, foxholes and tents. I lived in hotels, where there were paved roads and sidewalks, then in MACV complex, complete with an Olympic sized swimming pool. I didn't have bullets whizzing by my head. I didn't have buddies bleeding or spilling their guts over me. I can only imagine the pain that was felt. By the time that I saw you, your pain was all gone. All that was left was your dead rotting flesh.

Who was the enemy, them or us? What did it matter when they are dead?

I guess I never knew how popular "GARY" was. But that name is there on almost every panel. It could have been mine—*but it's not.*

(Rewritten from my journal of thoughts at the WALL in Washington D.C., 5/21-22/94.)
Gary T. Redlinski 57F, Graves Registration, identification specialist

"Der Opfergang"

Vaughn Stelzenmuller

German writer Rudolf Binding's fictional book by this title, meaning "The Great Sacrifice," was one of those boring college German-class stories we had to read. I hear it also had gotten made into an equally boring movie in Nazi Germany after Binding's death, but the *title* was great. The story did get me thinking about sacrifices made in daily life, especially in military days.

An early great chance for small sacrifice happened at ROTC summer camp rifle range. Picture cadet *Best*, "Buzz" as everyone called him, one of those good guys who also couldn't shoot worth two damns. Although worthwhile soldier-material in every other respect, Buzz grumbled loudly all day on my left at the range, running through our second day of marksmanship qualifications. Something, or someone else got blamed all day for his basically missing the half-barn-sized target 100 yards down range, consistently. Not wanting to finish off this final qualification day in too ill a humor, I knew something had to be done, or many of us would be hearing days' worth of complaints about Buzz's rifle, the ammunition, the weather, flying birds, whatever you think of.

Since I had done well qualifying both days, I vaguely knew I had a few shots to waste on trifles. On our second-last clip of M1 ammunition for the day, matters got worse. A call came back from down range that Buzz's shots may be "keyholing." Clearly, Buzz's shot must have hit a rock behind the target line, then ricocheted through the back of his target in a tired tumble. Unfortunately, Buzz picked up this new *keyholing*, and

Vietnam

started ranting about why ALL of his shots are wild, were wild, and always would be wild. His rifle, or the ammunition, or the world in general was making him keyhole his shots. God help us shut this man up! A cadet far down from Buzz's left called out, "Maybe it's your shooting, K*eyhole!*" That's too ugly. Buzz didn't deserve that.

Our lane instructors (LIs)—*real* Army privates and *real* corporals—crankily paced left and right along the firing line, making sure all was safe and non-cheating. Competent soldiers, but not an even match for us smartass ROTC cadets. I waited for our LI to be pacing away from me. Luckily, Buzz fired with regularity, probably jerking every shot with consistent, predictable, irregular aim. Timing myself with the LI's absence and Buzz's shots, I smoothly aimed left, squeezed off one round, then smoothly re-aimed straight downrange.

It likely seemed odd that I only showed seven holes on my target, after having such a lucky day otherwise. I could hear the scoring pits now: "Haaa, *lookit* Mr. Davy Crockett, Mr. Davy *Crawwwwwckettt*! Couldn't even hit the barn-sized board!"

What the heck, though, I can take it, and Buzz came up with a clean, miraculous 9-hit on his board, as shown by the scorer's paddle rising from the target line. Buzz was elated.

Then peace came over the range. Over the weekend, when we got an evening pass in town, and a group of us including Best sat munching giant steaks, no one talked about rifles. The weensy sacrifice paid for itself. Shame on me for not knowing if Buzz came out all right with whatever Vietnam assignment he ended up later. I trust it did *not* rhyme with "infantry"....

Still, this ROTC *thing* shouldn't be labeled an epic *Opfergang*. I didn't give up anything. It was for the selfish purpose of calming a buddy, and I'm here bragging about it 50 years later.

Three *Stripes*, and I'm *In*

Vaughn Stelzenmuller

Some unnamed, but well-recalled "buck" sergeant (shoulder rank on sleeve: three chevron stripes on top, no "rocker" stripes on the bottom; an Army enlisted rank of "E5") gave me a chance to not only *reflect*, but also *correct* at lightning speed.

During riot control training at Ft. Hood, Texas, preparing to deploy to a very unsettled *August-1968* Chicago if so ordered, here I was, second lieutenant leading one of the endless riot control formations in training. Most of this drill consisted of a moving wedge-shaped line formation of bayonet-fixed infantrymen, none of whom wanted to be there. Deploying against fellow American citizens never seemed like a just idea to any of us.

This three-stripe sergeant in the first rank (row), near the point of this wedge, had let his rifle sag a bit as we moved along solidly, deliberately, per the prescribed training. I smacked his rifle upward in an automatic shoulder-jerk reaction to bring his rifle barrel up. From his spot in formation, came this frightened, but determined, "Don't do that again, Sir!"

After a few seconds I realized that he had just taken a huge risk, speaking like that to an officer, so I had better take a risk, too. Besides, he was right! Striking his rifle in formation was like striking the man himself, as far as I *and* the Army were concerned.

Halting the formation, I announced in my best snippy, crispy second-lieutenant voice that I had just made a mistake.

"Here's how *we're* going to correct it!" barked the pompous, crisp-voiced second lieutenant. (Notice the "we").

I had this sergeant step forward and lead the training drills, and I took his rifle *and* place in the formation. An even swap. He and I were both, shall we say, apprehensive, and though the sergeant could afford to show it, I couldn't.

He did quite fine the rest of the training—how much can you mess up riot control training, anyway—and I did all right also, rifle, bayonet, and boots, and with crispy mouth shut. I only prayed that our company commander didn't step outside for a look. He was a through-the-ranks man who never showed much sense of humor, dry or otherwise, and probably would not like seeing one of his platoon leaders in drill line.

Who knows whether anybody else learned anything that morning, except for me? I had temporarily jogged myself *outside* approved Army behavior, and wish I had thanked that *three-stripe* sergeant for jogging me back *in*. But it likely didn't seem like something a crisp, snippy, pompous-ass second lieutenant was supposed to do. Hey, lieutenants learn pretty slow, so *one lesson at a time, please*!

Accidental Leadership Lessons at the Rifle Range

Vaughn Stelzenmuller

"You got range officer duty next week, Lieutenant," said the busy battalion operations officer, who just found an easy way out of the assignment himself, and who also outranked me "by one." All right, no panic. Read all the post and range rules and requirements, contact the Post Engineer office to confirm the date, coordinate the movement with all the company executive officers (or *far, far* better—the first sergeants).

After a short week of confirming arrangements, triple checking stuff, down to the range the *lucky* battalion soldiers go. Happy, happy soldiers! Another great day of rifle range! All the usual fiddling done, we finally get around to some actual shooting—today the M14 rifle would be the weapon of choice for qualifications, whether they needed it or not. Time to open fire. Open fire the line did.

Until, that is, the senior NCO hurried up to ask me, "Sir, there's some kind of odd movement downrange." Way, way downrange it looked like. Even though that movement seemed a blurry mile distant, that's at the so-called maximum effective range for the M14. Field glasses in hand, like a hero Civil War Union platoon leader looking for *screaming Rebs* on the horizon, I saw four trucks, *without* blur.

"*Schweizerscheissonbrot!*" my brain screamed to myself. My NCO, a good-looking dark-haired career sergeant, obviously hoping not to be tossed into the stockade later that evening, clearly also found the presence of a shielding officer useful.

"Cease fire! Cease fire!" I screamed, running left and right along the firing line, waving my arms like some novice Civil War Union hero platoon leader seeing those *scattering Rebs* starting to surrender yonder down the road. I did not feel much like a hero. "Remove your magazines, open your bolts, and place your rifles down in front of you, muzzles up and pointed down range!" Yeah, right, *down range*. I might as well have said *doom range*, for all the worth my career was now heading.

The next angry 20 minutes on the field commo line to the Post Engineer's office, done in my best imperial voice, uncovered another scheduled logistic activity which had briefly passed through the lower range at the time we riflemen showed up. As to why the post engineer let us begin in spite of this scheduling overlap? This had to do with my not, "Asking permission to 'open fire.'" We were supposed to go to a rifle range and peel carrots? *Ooh & ahhh* over the sunrise? Admire the terrain?

After another 20-minute delay, the post called to let us know that we could "Go ahead" with our range firing.

Oh, no you don't, you Post-Engineer double trickster. You lieutenant-testing *smart-aleck.* You smug, office-sitting, schedule-shuffling Post Engineer's office soldier-person! Calmly, I asked if we had "permission to open fire." Specifically. Exactly in those words. A bit of post-engineer chuckle came back with a short, "You may open fire."

Finishing the day without more mishap, the range control contingent headed back to battalion by Jeep. That would be me, my dark-haired career sergeant, a junior non-career NCO, and our conscripted young PFC driver.

At which moment the battalion commander radioed me.

I rattled off the day's story, too much detail probably, including that part about how the post engineer's office said everything "ended satisfactorily." I could hear that colonel's brain grinding when he ended with, "Well, it's *not* satisfactory with me. I'll see you when you get back to battalion. OUT!"

Icicles must have frozen up the jeep, as three enlisted men made themselves as tiny and motionless as possible, not knowing what to say to this junior officer who just found himself very publicly in a very bad military spot.

Leadership sometimes takes place "on accident," as my little kids in future years might say it. After signing off to a dyspeptic battalion commander, I waited a couple beats, then calmly told the jeepload, "I suppose if *the enemy* was just listening in on the radio, they would have *no* trouble labeling which one of us was the boss."

"*Which one was the boss*?! *Waa-a-a-a-a-a, ha-ha-ha-ha-ha!*" That joke broke the icicles with its Swiss-army-knife meanings, and the rest of the ride back got spent with each of my riders howling with laughter over each other about the roughest and *worst-est* thing that ever happened to *them* in their time with the Army. Three of us ended the day less tense and troubled, and the remaining one of us—the officer in deep military trouble—never did get called in by that battalion commander.

Textbook Soldier

Vaughn Stelzenmuller

We're not talking "Rhinestone Cowboy" here. Rather, this happy romance tale, between a hard-at-work younger soldier and his older engineering texts, tells that storybook reunion umpteen thousand miles away from college.

For some reason, I felt a growing wish to go back through a couple of my engineering books, from smack in the middle of the Vietnam highlands. A very fortunate and grateful graduate of the first Army ROTC two-year scholarship program at my college, I would partly pay back school and country by working this assignment in 1969 Vietnam. Oddly, I missed a couple of those engineering textbooks. The one I thought I missed most, my basic thermodynamics text (*thermo* for short), had one of those titles easy to forget. In distant second place was an irritating text titled *Momentum, Heat and Mass Transfer*, by Bird, Stewart and Lightfoot. *Bird, Stewart and Lightfoot* for short, if I absolutely had to. It could double as a great doorstop.

Yes, although you do miss wife and mother and father during overseas military duty, the Army can't mail those good people to you. As consolation, you *can* sometimes get your books air-delivered. And airdropped they were, less gently than a future Amazon drone could, onto a green jungle-style hillside.

Per usual "lieutenant's bad luck," this airdrop dropped bullet-like just over the outside edge of a large military operation on an achingly beautiful green patch of mountain range in Central Vietnam, when advising a company of very agile Vietnamese Montagnard infantry scouts. The helicopter pilot radioed ahead that he would be dropping my books in this idyllic dangerous nowhere, along with a small sack of prime steaks. Those Vietnamese scouts got to the drop zone athletically, seconds ahead of me, and then promptly brought me—my books. That evening around a cooking fire, my scout buddies passed around excellent small cuts of prime "water buffalo." What the heck, I got my books *and* a bite of my steak, and no one had gotten killed that day.

Even years later I put up with the howling laughter from my now-less-agile Army buddies about my getting "physics" books flown in *gratis* for the Army's special-pet soldier boy, compliments of the American taxpayer. To temper my anguish, they would buy me a drink or two. Thermodynamics paid off.

During a couple Army moves later, those two world-traveling textbooks disappeared, along with other assorted items in a military "*oops* cloud" (odd how the military never seems to send you *extra* items). *Bird, Stewart and Lightfoot* was not missed. The *thermo* book, yes. I wish I could remember the title.

Dak To encampment, many times in the path of North Vietnamese Army (NVA) invasions

"Praise the Lord, and Pass the Coffee"

Vaughn Stelzenmuller

One morning at a veterans' writing session, a take-charge veteran member brought us each cups of coffee as we busily tried to compose from a set of writing "prompts." That setting recalled an important time where delivery of coffee to the "front" was as important as bringing ammunition.

The hot coffee cup that morning for-real took me back smack into a no-moon night in a small godforsaken Army compound in Nowhere, Central Highlands, Republic of Vietnam, a half century ago. Especially way out in Upper Nowhere, junior officers got assigned nighttime duty officer rotations. You know, where this duty officer is totally responsible for every damned thing "that happens or fails to happen at the post" overnight.

My first rotation, this almost lightless night, turned out to be one of those where our G-2 (military intelligence) had just warned us of imminent local NVA (North Vietnamese Army) concentrations. Making the rounds of the several compound guard towers, I could see these soldiers manning the towers, drafted *kids* actually, were clearly edgy to the point of terrified. These grown-up boys, standing alone, eyes desperately trying to separate shades of shifting blackness and squirmy motion several hundred yards out, wanted to be anywhere else. I quite understood, and personally wished they—*draftees*—didn't have to be stuck in this deadly spot either.

An idea! The compound mess sergeant, fortunately not the most organized personality, had left a covered half-cauldron of un-dumped dinner coffee in the small mess hall kitchen. I found the stove, fired that baby up, and in 15 minutes had reasonably warmed drinks ready to go. I didn't mind looking like a waiter, disguised as a first lieutenant in fatigues, walking around the perimeter like one of those *Octoberfest babes* hauling steins of Munich's finest brew in each fist. I climbed each guard tower, mug in hand, in order of the most exposed towers first.

The way those kids greeted me, you would have thought I was one of the Beatles! Actually, they were greeting the mugs of warm printers-ink swill more than me, but *somebody* had to be the delivery boy. They were greatly surprised and pleased, and that made *me* less scared. I did not tell them that.

The coffee and the brief chatting clearly took some edge off the night. To make sure that they kept plenty of focused *edge*, though, I reminded each one to "keep a sharp eye out," and to have their ammunition bandoliers close. "Everybody in there," I drawled, nudging my elbow toward the sleeping compound behind us, "is counting on you." Or something Charles-Bronson-like. I really, really meant it. I suspected, though, that passing the coffee cup got more praise than passing the *5.56* ammunition, at coal-black 2:00 AM.

Tan Khanh USMACV Base, hunkered down

A Tale of Two Horribles

Vaughn Stelzenmuller

I really doubt that even very many seasoned soldiers have seen a B40 (RPG, rocket propelled grenade) shell in flight. After having assaulted a medium-sized mountain and then busy securing the crest with an advance of Vietnamese Scouts, I had the strange experience of glancing upwards in a micro flash at the underside of one of those rockets streaking overhead. Unfortunately, two of my Montagnard scouts also saw that rocket, and then bolted in panic rearwards, same direction as the B40 round was going.

I didn't run. But I *did* freeze. And I looked behind me. It's the same effect as running.

Yes, I knew what I should have done—drop prone toward the enemy fire and prepare to "receive the threat to the front with deliberate defensive fire." In English: hit the ground fast and get ready to shoot front, fast. That hesitation, loss of momentum, indecision could have gotten me killed for starters, and those behind me, for finishers.

The second horrible story had happened 10 minutes earlier—maybe it was 10 hours—where I had behaved the exact opposite. It should have been fun to tell this happy tale of being present at the "birth" of an American artillery firebase, and then its "retirement" a few weeks later. Nothing like that interested me on that raw mountaintop the day of the airmobile drop to secure the ground for the firebase. Seeing an unsuspecting enemy to the front, I ran forward, this dumbass *John Wayne* firing away.

Can you see why this impulsive rush mirrors the impulse to *stop* moving later that day? Exact opposite situations, but exact-same reactions. Both went against training, both stopped crucial thinking, and both could have got me killed deader than those gray boulders around me. And yes, I should have done the same thing as before: hit the ground and get ready to shoot. Freezing in place or charging forward—both impulses come from the *same* brain cells. Not often do I stumble on a biological insight like that. After the fact, of course. Dumbass.

There is a long-term happy ending to the story, of course, because I am still here mouthing about it. It does make me shake my head how I committed both sides of that great insight days later, the last hour of the last day of that firebase's life. We didn't really *retire* it like I said earlier, the Army just *got up 'n left* the spot.

Headquarters radioed to ask what US persons were left to take that last look-around for sensitive items left on the firebase. I heard that same bozo *John Wayne* briskly barking through *my* own lips and into *my* radio that, "*Of course* I would volunteer to stay." Headquarters helpfully volunteered in return that, "Your ride will be back shortly." In English: "We'll get you out soon as we can. Weather may be closing in."

Mr. John Wayne here didn't realize how quiet an abandoned firebase could be, surrounded by kilometers of lush hiding spots. Yes, I checked through the perimeter, always looking around at the horizon—all four of them at the same time in fast blurs. My blurry brain did appreciate how, no doubt, why an average rich person, in better times, would eagerly pay thousands of dollars for a vacation to such an exotic overlook.

Then 10 hours later—maybe it was 10 minutes—a UH-1 Huey helicopter flew in low, landing by-the-book close to the white smoke marker I tossed out to the old landing pad. I *could* brag that I was the "last man standing" on that hilltop, but a more accurate helicopter crewmen's view would have described me as, "Last man sprinting like hell." No freezing up this time.

A Call for Help, from 1969

Vaughn Stelzenmuller

You out there! *Ye* veterans of the Vietnam era, even *ye non-veterans* from that time—please think. Think! What ingredients did those scoundrelly, wonderful pill factories make the Contac™ cold medication from back then? If you know, please write and tell me, and I'll be your friend for life for a month!

On a scale of 0-to-17, this cry for help rates an urgency of about "2." This one's a great "2," though, because it has excellent value for the next time this veteran gets a really bad cold. For *your* head, too! The question is OTC-drug related, but calls for superman/woman memory: what pharmaceutical did Contac™ have in it, circa 1969, which gave it such a punch?

You see, picture this 23-year-old Army stud in the western end of *Nowhere*, Vietnam, who one sunny subtropical afternoon caught what we called The Creeping Crud (upper respiratory version, that is), which was really some kind of godawful plague-strength head cold. The military compound doctor took me to the compound hospital complex, which consisted of two sleeping bags in the tactical operations center, which in turn consisted of two large tents, and then made me swallow two capsules labeled "Contac™" at about 2000 hours (8 p.m., local civilian time). Next thing I saw, Vietnam was happily operational at *0800 hours* (8 a.m., local civilian time) 12 hours later, next day. Sunny! Nobody shooting. No ugly head cold! Miracle! Holy *malacrollymelinda*! *What was in that masked medication?*

One suspects that administering *two* of those 1969-version tabs would not be allowed today, maybe never. The compound doctor, wise beyond his really-old 27 years, would have known that such pharmaceutical dosages would either cure or kill, but was almost certainly betting on a cure rate better than 50-50. One never knew when the compound would need that extra rifle-bearer at 0430 hours in *Western Nowhere*, Vietnam.

Nevertheless, HELP! Does anyone out there know the active ingredient in 1969 Contac™? Having badgered the Contac Corporation (or whatever they fell under those days) with several phone calls and emails, I found three kinds of company Contac-contacts, all of whom gave me zero information:

1. Persons too young to know, or to figure out what my phone call was all about.
2. Persons of medium age who couldn't give three flying feathered figs over what my phone call was about.
3. Persons of wiser age who spotted a future legal liability when they heard one, and who knew *exactly* what my phone call was about.

None of these Contac-contacts added a whit to my knowledge. It was a total *pooh-pooh* from American industry.

So please...anyone,... ?

Homecoming

Vaughn Stelzenmuller

"One of the myths of the Vietnam War was people spitting on returning Viet Nam veterans in large mass." So wrote David Sirota, a syndicated columnist whose essays I particularly dislike, in one of his pieces a couple years ago or so. He does have a point here, though. Such a disgusting thing never happened to me, or to anyone I actually know, even indirectly. Oh, of course these things happened. Fortunately not in huge numbers. On the other hand, we rarely received what might be called a *thank-you handshake* either. One could say the receptions were more like, "Well, just another one of those returning soldiers."

My first citizen greeting upon landing at Los Angeles airport turned out to be a gent who asked me for a quarter. Or maybe it was a dollar, or a sawbuck. Or anything more solid than the time of day. Still, he was an American, and without a firearm, and that was a good thing.

About one and one-half hours into the draggy wait at the terminal, I found myself offering a cigarette to a crazy-haired woman who faked sanity by air-diagramming how the Army destroyed stuff with their "cobalt bombs." She didn't really hate the Army, and she did appreciate the *Lucky Strike*, and I'm telling you the humorous tale now. It felt good later, though, to buy a *Time Magazine* at the sundries counter. It wasn't out-of-date.

You can imagine the physical relief hours later from sitting back in my aisle seat, airborne over California and pointed east. That Army uniform tended to let people leave you pleasingly to yourself, if they weren't crazy.

Vietnam

Now, when the Army paymaster kicked you out of country at Tan Son Nhut Airbase, Republic of Vietnam, he did so with tens and twenties. Back then, buying an inflight two-dollar scotch & ice with a *ten* made a problem for the flight attendant. She told me that she would collect from me on the way back, after she got some change.

Ten minutes later, as she slender-hipped past me on the way to serving first class again, I reminded her that I still had a two-dollar debt to society, *and* United Airlines to pay.

"Oh, no sir," she told me, professional-voiced, "Two gentlemen back there took care of it."

Turning around, I saw these two well-dressed businessmen, not young, but not particularly old either, and neither very white nor very black, raising their own airlines-plastic cups to me. I raised mine, nodding my most appreciative thanks. I was home.

1970s AND 1980s

A Military Homefront Experience

Sue Spitulnik

According to the National Conference for State Legislators, only 7.6% (in 2019) of all Americans have ever served in the United States military. I beg to differ because I was a dependent wife and had two children. No, I didn't serve to the extent of following orders and being asked to brandish a weapon, but I served by being the back-up, the home front, who gave up my childhood roots, and never gave them to my kids, then willingly packed and moved each time the Air Force ordered my ex-husband to do so. I made immediate friends with new neighbors and relied on other members of my husband's unit as family because I had no other choice. This was during the 1970s when computers and smart phones didn't exist, so I wasn't able to email my family or provide Facetime for my children with their grandparents. We waited for a snail-mail letter and cried because we couldn't hear the voice of the person who wrote the words.

As I look back now, as a grandmother, I could easily be categorized as one who "joined the military" to escape my teenage situation. My mother died of cancer when I was a senior in high school after suffering for three years. My father was an alcoholic, which was never discussed while my mother was alive. Living with him when he was drinking had become unacceptable. I started college, but when my high school sweetheart enlisted in the Air Force to avoid being drafted into the Army during the Viet Nam wind-down, I followed him and got married. I was 18-1/2, thought I knew what the world was all about, and felt ready to tackle being a wife and mother. Now I can see how naive I was. At the time, I found it exciting to live in new places, meet different people, anxiously wait to hear what base we would be assigned to, and get a passport to travel over-seas. In the seven and a half years our marriage lasted, we lived in four different states and spent three years in England, living in three different towns around Lakenheath AFB, 70 miles north of London.

My transient lifestyle was made apparent to me when I returned to my rural New York state hometown area for my 25th high school reunion. Drink chips were given away for being the last person to have your hand up at the end of questions like: how many addresses have you had since high school; have you lived in another country; how many states have you lived in? I ended up with five of the chips. It might sound like all the moving was a bad thing, but in retrospect it wasn't. Some of my fellow students had never left our home town and the puddle they lived their lives in was very small. My puddle had been turned into not just a big lake, but an ocean. I had experienced things like having dinner in London and on top of the Space Needle in Seattle, driving cross-country in the US, experiencing various customs, and having a Medal of Honor winner as a personal friend. Becoming a military dependent totally changed my life.

Our last duty station as a married couple was in Tacoma, WA, where my ex-husband was assigned to McChord AFB which was relatively small. Right down the road was Ft. Lewis Army Post, which was huge. I started working at the Denny's right outside of McChord's gate in 1979 and shortly after that, got divorced. I continued to work at Denny's until 1991. Most of my customers were somehow connected to the military: either active duty, retired career military, people who had served a few years, and their dependents who understood what serving in the US military can do to a person, especially those who serve on the front lines during wartime. Many of my co-workers were military dependents and they arrived with their spouses and left with them. Long term friendships just didn't happen because of reassignments of the active duty members.

Of all the people I met while working at Denny's, four stand out. An Army chaplain named Gary Adkinson became a trusted confidant across the counter. He had been stationed in Korea and while there, fell in love with a beautiful lady whom he had to leave behind when he rotated back to the states. He had learned to write her language and would sit at the counter and write her long letters while we kept his coffee cup full. He did this for months while waiting for the paperwork and red-tape to be worked through so she could immigrate to the States. The day finally arrived that he flew back to Korea to bring home the woman he thought would spend the rest of her life with him. We welcomed her at Denny's like it was our brother returning with his bride. I don't remember the exact timing, but she left Gary for another man. I never dared ask if he felt she had used him to get her green card, but I did ask him how he could deal with it after being faithful to her during all the months he waited. His answer was something to the effect, if you love somebody, you have to allow them to be free. I know it hurt him deeply but he handled it with grace. I hated when he transferred away, and I lost my "brother" to talk to.

The Medal of Honor winner that I had the privilege of knowing was Delbert Jennings. Often when a new face appeared at the counter I learned his first name and memorized his breakfast order. It was later their rank and which branch of service they were in became known. I've never been much of a hero-worship type person and I treated Del like I did any other person I waited on. That was the secret to our friendship. One day there was a funeral for a high-ranking officer stationed at Ft. Lewis that anybody who was somebody attended. Del came into Denny's afterward in his dress greens with his Medal of Honor on. A man who had been in the Army, who was then an insurance salesman, zeroed in on that medal and asked me to move his coffee down next to Del. They talked for some time. The insurance man finally left for an appointment. Del told me later that occurrence was why he rarely let anyone know about his award. He explained that medal was only bestowed on someone when there had been a whole lot of blood and lives lost. He didn't feel like a Vietnam hero who had saved some lives, he felt like a loser who let the guys down that didn't make it home. And anyone that saw the medal wanted the gory details of what he had gone through to have his name submitted for the honor. The memories were not good ones, but as the owner of the medal it was his job to wear it with distinction, which I saw him do. Currently I use Medal of Honor forever postage stamps. If you buy a full sheet, you can find Del's name on the list. I wish his picture would have been included. He died in Hawaii where he was stationed when he retired from the Army.

The insurance agent I mentioned was named Jim Derck. I dated Jim for a time and it was then, dealing with his nightmares and survivor guilt, that I learned the reality of what front line action can do to a man. It was his job to assign reconnaissance helicopters to fly into the DMZ to drop supplies and remove wounded. I don't recall the year he was in Vietnam, it doesn't matter much. It fell on his shoulders to make the assignments as to whose turn it was to fly to which sector on a given day. The crux was, for a couple of weeks, there was a specific sector that the helicopters didn't make it back from. In his words, he had to choose who was going to die that day. He never got over feeling it was his fault some didn't survive. Del tried to impress upon him he was fulfilling an assignment/order and nothing more, but when a man has a heart as big as Jim's, that doesn't hold much water. He was often suicidal and who can blame the guy. I wonder today if he is still alive.

One other man I remember well is John Arrowood. He was retired Army and had a full head of white hair. Whenever his wife or three daughters wanted him for any reason, they would come to Denny's in search of him. Remember, this is before cell phone days. John was at the counter all hours of the day, and nights when he couldn't sleep. I never heard the reason behind his not sleeping well so I don't know if it was war-related or not. I do remember all of us, about twelve ladies from the age of 25 to 40, talked to John about car problems, kid and boyfriend/husband troubles and what Army posts were better than others. I often thought he spent more time listening to our troubles than he did his own three daughters. I had known him for about eight years when he changed from regular coffee to decaf. I thought it had something to do with the sleeping problem. Then he started coming in irregularly and losing weight. I should have caught the signs, but I didn't. His oldest daughter came in after he had been missing for a few weeks to let us know he had died of leukemia. Six of us went to his funeral and cried like we had lost our own father. I wrote his family a poem that all his hours away from them were not wasted because they were our gift.

As I write, so many names and memories come back to me. At the time I still didn't have a good understanding of what some of the Vietnam vets had gone through. Today I can picture the faces I knew back then and know they were dealing with the demons of war. I wish I could have been more supportive with the right word or touch of understanding instead of keeping their coffee cups full, sharing a joke and remembering their names.

I left Washington State and returned to western New York State in 1991 when my father was diagnosed with cancer for the second time. It was time to come home. Dad lived for six months after I got back. He was married at the time to a woman I didn't care for. In fact we got a card from his long-time poker playing friends, that they wouldn't attend any service for him as long as she was involved; my three older sisters and I weren't surprised. Anyway, during those six months I can honestly say Dad and I became friends. He admitted he knew how much his alcoholism had adversely affected our family. I accepted his admission but didn't voice any forgiveness. I visit his and my mother's graves on his birthday and leave each of them a rose in their favorite color. I am finally realizing how much power my mother's early death had over my life. For one thing, I don't think I would have quit college had she been alive and all that I'm writing never would have happened. I digress.

In 2013, I sat down at my computer to start writing a story that had been rattling around in my head for some years. It's a soap opera type family saga set in Tacoma, Washington, and one of the main characters is a young man that becomes an Air Force pilot against his father's expectation causing a huge family rift. So I could accurately portray my character's life I needed to find an Air Force pilot I could interview. My search led me to the Rochester Veterans Writing Group in 2015. I not only found a pilot, I found Chuck Willard who, during the Vietnam era, flew the exact airplane I was showcasing. He has spent hours editing my work, making suggestions for improvement, and checking details. His friendship is invaluable to me. The story turned into a long novel that is yet to be published. It may never be, but the exercise brought me back into a group of people who understand the military way of thinking and life experience.

The writing group meets once a month and I have only missed a few meetings since I started attending. This is important because being around "my" vets has brought me home to a feeling I didn't know I was missing until I experienced it. I found my "tribe" of brothers and sisters that "get it." If you have never had a military member in your family, or experienced living a military life, you won't understand the meaning of tribe. When the group sits around the table and writes memoirs from thought provoking prompts, we are each remembering our personal experiences. Once the allotted time for writing is up, we read aloud our musings, sharing the memorable highs and lows, and sometimes comical, points of military life. It's a healing process and only safe to do with other vets who understand: the front lines come with blood, gore and death; the military comes with pride, service, boredom and chaos; the home front can be supportive or fall away in a flash; and it takes 22 to 25 other members in the background to support the ones brandishing weapons no matter the circumstances. Because of that fact, if you mention in front of me that a military veteran doesn't deserve to be called a veteran unless they have served in wartime front lines you will get a really strange look and a loud argument.

It's these men's reality that has kept me on the far side of the reflecting pool to admire the Vietnam Memorial Wall in DC. I get too emotional to get any closer. There are some names on the wall from my hometown area and names I have been introduced to through friends that made it home. I was too young to get involved in the war protests at the time they were taking place and too young to grasp the lies our government was telling us about the situation. The takeaway from that is I don't trust any politicians when it comes to what they say out loud. There have been too many instances proven that what they are doing behind closed doors doesn't match what they are telling the American people. If you have the opportunity to watch the documentary, *Vietnam* by Ken Burns, that last statement will become clear to you. What our guys suffered was needless and inhuman, as was what the other side suffered as well. Forgive me for focusing on Vietnam. That was my era. And I'm sorry I'm not mentioning any ladies, it's only because they aren't the ones that I got to know personally.

* * *

For this project the group decided to tell stories that were especially for our families and to share the history of some people that affected our lives. I have shared the latter, so will now back up and tell you about daily life as a military wife. It wasn't all that different from a non-military wife's except we were told where to live and we didn't question the fact our husband might not be home for weeks at a time if he was gone for training or to a temporary duty station. There were a couple of tricky parts to being separated as a married couple. The spouse at home had to "be in charge" of everything and make all the decisions for the house, the kids, the car, etc., then the spouse would return and who was "in charge" could easily become a power struggle between the two. Loneliness was a common problem especially since there was no immediate family nearby to spend time with. Some wives couldn't handle the extended family separation and went home to Mama.

Like I said in the beginning, I married my high school sweetheart, Sheldon, better known as Shady, while he was attending radio school at Keesler AFB in Biloxi, MS, February, 1972. The married guys were allowed to live off base but had to report to the barracks in the morning and march to school with the rest of their class. We lived on the fifth floor of an apartment building from where I could watch the formations making their way across base. He came home from school one day to tell me he had found out the radio guys were the first ones to be dropped into a war zone and he wasn't about to let that happen to him. Going to Vietnam was still a possibility so he soon failed out of school and was assigned to the base supply squadron at Plattsburgh AFB in upstate New York. His job would be fueling airplanes. We had decided to have our children on "Uncle Sam's Nickel," so I was five months pregnant when we moved. Our son was the last boy born in the base hospital maternity ward. Starting March 1, 1973, the pregnant military members and dependents had their babies in the local hospital. We liked Plattsburgh. It was the weather we were used to, and we were only six hours from home.

Wherever we lived there were extra guys at our dinner table. I liked to cook, and I liked company. In Plattsburgh it was common to have three or four eating spaghetti, not at dinner time, but after the local bar closed. Shady had simple food tastes; spaghetti consisted of cooked noodles with a can of Hunts tomato sauce on them. Disgusting! I could spend all day making sauce with onions, peppers and meat and he would refuse to eat it. Making spaghetti the way he wanted it was quick, so feeding extras was no problem. The visitors didn't care about the quality of the sauce either, it wasn't mess hall food and it was free, besides they all had a snoot full when they wolfed it down. Home baked cookies and cakes disappeared quickly too. I still remember all their names and wonder where they are now. To this day I rarely eat spaghetti.

At that time, each Air Force member had to do at least one out-of-country assignment during his four-year enlistment. Shady could have chosen an unaccompanied tour of one year, or accepted an accompanied tour and extend long enough to make it work timewise, which amounted to adding a year to his enlistment. We chose the latter and he got orders for Lakenheath AFB, in England. When he left the States our son wasn't walking yet so Daddy missed that milestone in our son's life. I wanted our children two years apart so talked to my OB/GYN and stopped taking precautions just before Shady left. I had been told the chance of my getting pregnant in that time period was slim, but of course it happened. So once again, I traveled to our next base while being pregnant. Years later Shady would tell our daughter he never felt included in the decision to have another child, so he was unable to feel a closeness to her. Yeah, that's one of the reasons he's my ex. But, had we not been separated, that probably wouldn't have happened. That's military life for you; deal with it or let it break you. The reality is, serving your country takes a toll on the whole family.

During that time period the Air Force member had to get to his duty station and rent a suitable apartment or house for his spouse/family before travel arrangements could be made for the rest of the family. I can remember driving to Rome, NY, and finding my way around the Manlius military installation (now defunct) to get all the paperwork done. I felt so mature. My poor son had never had a babysitter before, and cried for half of the four hours I was away from him. It's not that we didn't believe in babysitters, it was we had never needed one. Being a stay-at-home Mom was one of the perks of being a military dependent. It was three months before my son and I traveled to England. At Mildenhall AFB when we were all finally reunited, my son and his father didn't recognize each other. Three months is a long time for an 18-month-old.

Our first home in England, located in the town of Brandon, Suffolk county, had a coal burning stove in the kitchen that also provided hot water heat to the other rooms via radiators. The two bedroom house with a fenced "garden" had been for rent for some time because of the heating system that few people knew how to handle. I loved that stove. There was also an electric stove, but all cakes, stews and roasts were cooked in or on the coal stove. One of our first purchases in England was a pram with large wheels, or in American, a baby carriage. We walked into town to go to the *chippy* (fish and chip shop), the greengrocer, the butcher and the public market on Saturdays. Of course, we did our major shopping on base at the commissary and Base Exchange, but incidentals we got locally. The temperature rarely went above 75 degrees or lower than 40 so walking was done all year round. Learning how to drive on the left-hand side of the road didn't seem to be a problem, but returning to the right side when I got back to the States took a bit more concentration for a time.

Not having immediate family close enough to depend on when a woman went into labor was acknowledged by the Air Force in England in 1974, so we were allowed to pick the date for our child's birth in order to line up babysitters for an older sibling or to let family know when to come visit. I believe my due date was December 15th. I don't remember why we picked the 11th, but my labor was induced and our daughter arrived with little effort on that day. She was a robust 8-pound baby until my milk came in, yes, breastfeeding was the "in" thing to do at the time, but then she started losing weight and throwing up. Turns out she was allergic to my milk and had some stomach issues as well. A few different formulas were tried before they found one she could keep down and start gaining weight again. She finally came home on January 3rd. Back then it was mandatory for the new mother and baby to stay in the hospital 72 hours. That was a blessing because that kept her in the nursery with immediate round-the-clock care. I can tell you, it's a sinking feeling to have a baby and go home without her in your arms. The military perk of medical coverage for the whole family saved us financially. There were no bills. I think we did have to pay a few dollars to have her birth recorded so we would have a legal birth certificate and a Certificate of Birth Abroad to ensure her American citizenship.

As Shady gained time in service and now with a second child, he qualified for base housing. Moving was a lark, a big truck pulled in, men wrapped your things carefully and deposited your stuff in the next location. You had to do your own unpacking and organizing. Darn it! The tough part was passing the cleanliness inspection when you moved out of any military abode. Most of us paid professional cleaners. It was worth it. We moved two times while in England. Each move brought new neighbors, a new pub to hang out at, a new town to walk in and the same APO address to hear from home. A unique part of "living inside the fence" of base housing was the freedom the children had. A mother was never quite sure where her child was when they went outside to play. Generally the closest playground was the spot to congregate. I'm not talking teenagers here, I'm referring to any child old enough and allowed to open the gate in their fenced yard. We left our doors ajar and sometimes your own kid would come in to use the bathroom and sometimes it was someone else's or a whole bunch of them would run through to get to the other side of the multi-family unit picking up a ball or other toy on the way through. Most of the moms knew all the kids and which house number they belonged to if any crying started. My son recounts a time when he was about 12 that his father told him he couldn't leave the base on his bicycle to go fishing in a nearby stream, so he rode to the other side of the base staying "inside the fence" to fish in a pond that was twice the distance away. Some of my children's escapades I'm glad I didn't know about at the time they took place.

While we were still in the house in Brandon, my Aunt Alda and my mother's best friend, Doris, came to visit for ten days. I knew Doris had been sick for some time but I assumed if her family let her come she was well enough to travel. I didn't know until later that her son was supposed to talk her out of getting on the airplane, but she was so excited, he didn't have the heart to do it. She started having trouble breathing the third day she was with us. I called the base hospital and they agreed to see her since she was only in the country as a guest. Unfortunately, she died that evening of a heart attack. The "fun" began when it was finally noticed she had never signed her passport. How she got through customs leaving the US and when she arrived in London without anyone catching that omission is still a mystery. It did create quite the red-tape mess as far as getting her remains returned to the US. I found out years later her family had a funeral a couple of weeks after the event with an empty casket and told only the adults in the immediate family the truth. I still don't know how long it took for her to actually make it home. I felt very guilty that she had died on my watch and thought her family would be angry with me, but they weren't. They knew she was fulfilling a life-long dream of traveling. Now that I'm thinking about it, I don't remember how her luggage got home. I had told her and Aunt Alda to pack warm clothes because summer in England was cooler than in western New York State, and didn't we have a week of 80-degree weather. They were boiling most of the time. Another unfortunate aspect of that experience was, I was asked if I wanted the Red Cross to notify her family. In my naiveté I thought they would have someone go in person to make the notification. They didn't. They called her daughter at home, who then had to pay to call me in England totally confused and shocked in order to get the sad details. May I make a suggestion: if you ever have something like that happen to you, call someone both you and your visitor know well and have that person make a face-to-face notification.

A fun memory of living in the UK was the language. I figured we would all be speaking English and I was lucky I wouldn't have to learn a new language in order to communicate. That's not quite how it worked. People who live in the UK speak proper English with different enunciations than Americans. I learned quickly that I spoke American with a lot of slang thrown in and it didn't match theirs. It took me about six months to be able to eavesdrop on a conversation and understand all the words. The last month I was there we were invited by a local victualer, pub owner, to go to one of their association's fancy multi-course dinners. As we arrived at the party, I was instructed to not ask out loud what any word meant so I didn't publicly embarrass the host. It was quite the affair, government officials wore sashes to show what office they held, and others wore medals. This paraphernalia was not removed once dinner ended and the dancing began. The servers all wore red coats and white gloves. We were not allowed to smoke until after the fourth course and there had been a proper toast to the Queen, the same queen who is still sitting 42 years later. See what I mean about my puddle of life being an ocean?

While stationed in England we became friends with a couple, Tom and Sue. Sue and I had our babies about the same time. While the Dads went to the pub together we stayed at our house with the babies, talking girl talk, enjoying a "cuppa" tea and watching British television which was much less censored than American TV. Nudity was common and sexual innuendo was rampant. It seemed that any comedian that had a well-known reputation was a cross-dresser. That would never have been accepted in the US. Actually, the fact sex was talked about was refreshing. Of all the military, both men and women, I met over the years, Sue is the only one I am still in touch with. She's one of those people you can go months without talking to and pick up right where you left off. I have to admit, it's mostly because she keeps the thread of conversation active. We still share our girly secrets and laugh about how ignorant we were when we thought we were so grown up.

When Shady's tour was done in England, our kids and I returned to our hometown area ahead of him and remained there until he returned and got settled at Chanute AFB in Illinois, where he went back to school to learn how to run and care for a flight simulator. I think the separation was about two months. My kids got to spend some time with extended family but were still too young to form any real bonds with them. They are indeed military brats. Even today when we sit around the dinner table, the comment comes out that they have no roots. My daughter especially tends to choose people older than herself to get close to as the ones her own age haven't experienced enough in life for her to find interesting. It's all about the size of their puddles.

Again in Illinois we had single guys who were taking the same classes as Shady around the beer cooler and grill. It was summertime. My kids always had "uncles" to roughhouse with and they loved it. My daughter had continued to have health problems and it was at this base, at the ripe old age of two and a half, she had her urethras re-implanted into her urinary bladder using the valves from a pig. I took my son to the base day-care center and sat at the hospital by myself during the four-hour procedure while Shady went to school. He told me if he missed a day of class it could set him back a major amount of time and they might fail him out, which he didn't want to happen this time. I didn't believe him then and still don't. Your life isn't your own when you wear a military uniform, but I'm pretty sure they would have made an exception if they knew his baby was having major surgery. Sitting alone was just the way it was for a military wife too new to a duty station to have made any friends. Funny, I'm now the one that sits quietly, for hours, with friends and/or family when they need moral support while in the hospital. I guess those hours alone that day in Illinois taught me patience I can now share with others.

I had driven from New York State to Illinois with two children when we moved there, and in October of 1979 I found myself driving with the whole family on to Washington State. Our destination, McChord AFB in Tacoma. That was the first time I made the drive cross-country. I remember some of the scenery, but that's about all. Once at our destination, we stayed in a hotel for a couple of weeks before finding a house to rent. Because of my daughter's surgery we all went at the same time so she wouldn't have a break in medical care if it were needed quickly. I am happy to say she didn't. Tacoma was the lowest rent area for the nicest accommodations I ever experienced. Having Mt. Rainier to look at daily, if the clouds cooperated, was never tiresome and I came to love the locale. It was a bonus that one could be in the bustle of downtown Seattle, hiking trails up on Mt. Rainier or walking on the peer in Westport, on the Pacific Ocean, in an hour's drive time from any place in Tacoma. If my extended family didn't live in Western New York State, I never would have left Washington.

About six months after we arrived, Shady and I went our separate ways. We found no solutions to our problems even after multiple sessions of marriage counseling and we felt it was better for our children to see us separately than witness the escalating turmoil. Our divorce brought my days as a military dependent to an end, but my job at Denny's gave me a way to serve our military and their families for 12 more years.

***

I now serve in a way that's all my own by making patriotic quilts and presenting them to my veteran friends. I learned to sew when I was in high school and made my first quilt during that time frame. A very simple set of different color squares sewn together to form a colorful, warm, useful blanket. I've been making quilts ever since and am very fortunate to have a 600 square foot sewing studio in my home with multiple sewing machines, many quilting rulers and tools, and yards and yards of fabric to "play with." I can't tell you how many quilts I've made; it's in the hundreds. Currently my passion is patriotic quilts which means they are red, white and blue with maybe a little beige or black thrown in. The stitching I do that holds the quilt top, batting and backing together is not close, nor fancy, on purpose so it keeps the quilt more supple to form around a body shape when used as a warm cover. I am proud to tell you my husband is often with me when I'm in a quilt shop. He carries the bolts of fabric I pick, chats with the person who cuts what I ask for, and pays for it knowing I am going to give it all away. He's a veteran too and his generosity keeps me occupied doing something I love, and gives him a silent way to say thank you as well. We make a good team.

Asking for Help

Rori Murrell

My reaction to today's prompt brought me up short. I identified that receiving, much less asking for, help was something I just don't do. It occurred to me that asking/receiving help of any kind is tempered by three things:

- Having been raised in a traditional Polish family where independence and a strong "work ethic" were daily fostered.
- Having been a PTSD/trauma therapist for 38 years, working exclusively with combat veterans and their families.
- Having been sole caregiver for four elderly family members until their death.

Having said that, it seems to follow that I tend to perceive offers of help/advice as negative judgement of my abilities. This, of course, is exacerbated by the complex of emotions associated with loss, fear, and most importantly perhaps, regret.

Yet—there was a time—in the Army, as part of a unit, that help of any kind was accepted and returned. There was a mutual mission to accomplish. There was a bond that formed. Perhaps it was, for me, the ultimate sensation of acceptance and belonging. It worked for me then; I wish I had it now.

Our lives are complex, our emotions are guarded.

"I've got your back.

I'll take care of mine."

A Desire to Serve

Rori Murrell

After three years in the U.S. Army as a non-commissioned officer, my dream became a desire to be a career officer. I went to college upon discharge and then applied for officer training School (OCS) at Lackland Air Base, Texas. Mid-training I was deprived of my dream because of a chronic illness.

The initial months after discharge were filled with anger, depression, and many hospital stops. I felt that I was "floating to nowhere," feeling there was no place to go. In time I came to realize that perhaps I didn't have to wear the uniform to serve. I struggled to find out how.

My first thought was to become a nurse and work in a VA hospital. Regrettably, my entrance into various nursing schools was denied because of the same chronic illness. I fell back into "no man's land" again, winding up working in a bookstore.

Time passed and I renewed my search for a place to serve. It is said that "the seeker finds." One day I did *find*, and I knew my path. Having been a psychology major in college, I began to explore my options, a slow disappointing process.

In 1980, my husband, also a veteran, and I attended a rally on behalf of the newly forming Veteran's Outreach Center. It quickly became a place for both of us to continue to serve. We became volunteers helping to raise money and rehab the house donated to the VOC by a wealthy Rochestarian. Soon after, I went to graduate school. I did an internship and was licensed as a social worker with a specialty in PTSD. At this time *post-Traumatic Illness* was not even listed in the DSM of identified diagnosis. I began to work clinically with combat veterans who had served in Vietnam.

These words might make it sound easy and swift. It was not. The details of that first year of employment are forever seared into my memory. Being female and a non-combatant in a truly male arena, I strove to be effective and accepted. I was tested, left out and teased.

Eventually, I managed to prove myself and became the Clinical Director of the VOC. Though not initially accepted, I came to "belong." The VOC during this time was the only place in Rochester dealing exclusively with the Veterans of Vietnam. The Vet Center of the Veterans Administration was modeled on the VOC experience. We did good work and were proud of it.

After 20 plus years, the "bean counters and suits" took over the VOC administration. They eliminated PTSD and readjustment counseling to focus on such areas as housing, training, and substance abuse. I and my staff of two full-time and two part-time therapists were fired.

Once more ... adrift. But I was proud of the work we had done. We led the way and the path was true. The VA, sometime after, contacted me and made me an offer I couldn't refuse; to continue my work with combat veterans. Years later, I still, after retirement, continue to be available for phone calls and pro-bono work as needed.

The path and dream continue.

Day Care

Joe Mele

On a cloudy, cool and rainless fall day, I continued my search for work and responded in person to a help wanted ad for drivers. I was looking for something to fill in between "real" jobs. The trees and shrubs of the Day Care Center were taking on autumn colors, blending with the buff brick of the building. As I drove up to the entrance, I saw an elderly man shuffling out the front door, his pants around his ankles. He didn't get far before he was gently coaxed back inside by a middle-aged woman in a nurse's uniform.

I ignored the omen and proceeded to apply for and secure a position driving a passenger van for the center. Shifts were distributed among four or five different drivers. The route might vary day to day to accommodate a new client, or a sick one, or a changed schedule. The number of passengers on a run could vary from one to eight. The clients needed care for a variety of reasons: developmental or physical disability, dementia, and injury among them.

One Saturday morning, two of us were sent to pick up one patient at her home. The other driver, Paulo, was about my size—roughly 5'9" and 140 lbs. His English was heavily accented. My Spanish was non-existent. Until we got there, I didn't know why two of us were sent.

At the house, we walked up the first set of six steep brick steps, made a left turn on a landing, and up six more steps to the front door where an aide greeted us. We were brought into the front hall and introduced to the lady of the house who was sitting in a double wide wheelchair. I estimated chair and rider to weigh roughly 400 lbs. There was no ramp. Paulo grabbed one handle of the wheelchair, and I the other. We leaned the chair back and pushed it toward the front door and down the single step at the threshold, jarring the rider as the chair landed. Slowly, warily we approached the brick staircase and inched the chair forward over the first step until it started to drop, then held on desperately to prevent it from careening down all the steps at once. With the chair balanced precariously on the second step, Paulo and I glanced at each other and started laughing. We couldn't stop. At each step we laughed in the face of death—not our death—our client's. She started laughing too. We were crying by the time we made it to the van—unscathed. I spied no religious symbol, just a faded VFW decal starting to peel away from the back of her chair, but I know her survival was a miracle.

How she made it back up those steps and into her house, I never found out, but the next time she was picked up, Paulo and I did not get the call.

IRAQ, AFGHANISTAN, OTHER PLACES

War Zones

Janice Priester-Bradley

The loud noise over my head seemed unreal, but I had to keep telling myself *you are in a war zone*. War zones are not much to be afraid of—its places filled with fighting—objects flying back and forth that light up the sky in different colors, making sounds that spark the air.

War zones are not much to be afraid of. They are places where you are welcomed, but never able to come out and greet your neighbor.

War zones are not much to be afraid of. They are places of peace, serenity and surrender which capture our minds to believe *I am free*.

War zones are not much to be afraid of. They are places my spirit laid at rest.

Laid at rest against the loud noises in every head, causing reality.

How to Heal a Wound

Janice Priester-Bradley

It was a matter of time for the bleeding to stop, covering a soldier's arm with heavy pressure dressing pads as he watched me take his arm, preparing it for the healing process. This process takes time; did this soldier's arm have it? Well, I can say no one really knows how long, because a wound can be deep, a wound can be resurfaced, a wound can be placed as never going away...like a broken heart.

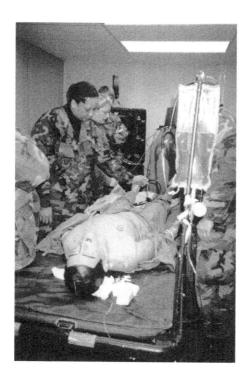

Costs

Janice Priester-Bradley

Let it be understood a cost is something one must pay.

It is the burden of paying for something wanted or desired.

The cost on African American ancestors' slavery had a cost,

but by staying united, gave them what they deserved today:

their freedom!

Hard to believe, but I found such a personal cost to pay, even in our modern military. Freshly commissioned into the medical service of the U.S. Air Force, I was stunned to have a superior officer telling me that I would never rise above the rank of *captain*. Fortunately, that odd officer never got in the way of promotions that I went on to earn:
It's *Colonel* to you now, Buddy!

Loss

Janice Priester-Bradley

To me, the word lost means you were found.

You have been psychologically, physically and socially rewarded and the freedom to move yourself into a different dimension of whatever paradise you want to pursue, I should say.

In this perspective you can say what you want, do as you please or even go where you never have gone before.

Come with me my veteran friend, take the journey of being lost.

I will not find you—ever.

Rollover Training

John Steele

One of the tasks that had to be completed before leaving Fort Lewis was rollover training. One of the more dangerous situations for military members here in Iraq is if the vehicle they are riding in rolls over. Of course, if IED's (Improvised Explosive Devices) are the reason the vehicle is rolling over, the IED is the bigger danger. However, with rollover, the injuries and deaths can be, and have been, minimized with knowing what to do in the event of a rollover. Thus, we have rollover training.

The training we had at Fort Lewis taught us what to do in the event of a rollover while in a Humvee. They have this training simulator which is built to replicate the inside of the Humvee. And then they can spin it. And by spin it, I mean slowly rotate, very slowly, about the speed of a hot dog that's been cooking for who-knows-how-long on the rotating grill at the 7-11. If ever there is a true rollover, it is going to spin considerably faster. But slow is a good way to start off the training.

Prior to getting in the simulator, we are taught what we have to do. First, we have to yell, "ROLLOVER!" three times. Why three times? I have no idea. If you are in a vehicle that is starting to roll over, yelling to warn everyone is a great idea. If you are in a vehicle that is in the process of rolling over, by the time you have yelled "ROLLOVER" once or twice, everyone in the vehicle is innately aware that it is rolling over, even if they hadn't heard you.

I actually jumped the gun a little. Even prior to that, everyone has to be strapped in, especially the gunner in the turret. Then as you yell "ROLLOVER!" three times, there are three more things you have to do simultaneously. The two people in the back seat of the Humvee have to hold on to the guy in the turret to prevent him or her from flying out of the vehicle. Everybody has to try to brace themselves. As you are rolling around, you don't want to be bouncing off everything. So you brace your legs and extend your arms and brace them against the roof or whatever you can to prevent yourself from becoming a projectile. If you are the driver, you brace your legs, and maintain control of the steering wheel. You can brace yourself somewhat with the steering wheel, and you don't want to let go if you have a chance to maintain control of the vehicle. And finally, everyone has to secure their weapons. As you are rolling around in a container, you don't want weapons and other large items to be flopping around, banging into you. Most of the injuries from rollovers are from flying debris within the vehicle, or the soldiers becoming flying debris inside the vehicle. Most of the fatalities in rollovers are from people becoming flying debris outside the vehicle.

Once the vehicle is done rolling, you then have to determine the best way to egress the vehicle, and then exit. Part of that involves unbuckling yourself while either upside down or at a ninety-degree angle, so best bet is to brace yourself. Sounds easy, doesn't it?

When we did the practical exercise, we didn't have anyone in the turret, which made it easier. We had a driver and a passenger in the front seat, and two passengers in the back seat. I was the driver, of course. We piled into the Humvee, strapped ourselves in, and started rolling. Everyone yelled "ROLLOVER" three times. It sounded like recess on the last day of school. Everyone was yelling, not in unison, and the whole thing was a big loud blur.

We had rubber duckies, which are fake hard rubber M-16 rifles. They didn't want the real things slamming into us. But everyone held their weapon, and no one got hit by a stray weapon that was bouncing around. (I almost used the term "loose cannon"). However, the cadre also had a fake, rubberized fire extinguisher tumbling around inside, which hit me once. It didn't hurt a whole lot, just enough, but it hammered home the importance of keeping the vehicle clean and secure. The cadre had a number of rubberized items that would repeatedly descend upon us in our rotisserie.

So we are spinning around like the wheel on the Wheel of Fortune, and when we stopped rolling, we were upside down. Not a problem. I know exactly what to do. I set my weapon down on the floor (roof) above my head. It is a very tight area, so I had to maneuver to put the weapon down. I brace myself, pressing my arms above my head, pushing against the roof which is under me. Well...wait a minute...how do you unbuckle your seat belt if your arms are bracing yourself so you don't fall as your strap releases you? My right hand is my dominant hand, so I will brace myself with my right arm, and undo the buckle with my left. Now I am currently suspended upside down by the seat belt. My weight in uniform is about 230 pounds, IBA (Interceptor Body Armor) is 47 pounds, helmet is another 9 pounds; there is close to 300 pounds being suspended and held in place by the tension in the seat belt. So simply hitting the button with my left hand isn't doing it. I am *not* releasing. Here is my disturbing thought process: "Consciously press harder with the left hand, no brace hard with the right hand, no, I have to do both at the same time. This button is harder than I thought. Press harder with the left. Don't loosen up the right, press on the roof with the right hand too so you don't fall on your head. This still *ain't* working. Switch. Brace with the left, get the buckle with the right. The left arm isn't going to be able to hold 300 pounds all by itself. Okay, quick with the right hand on the buckle, then back up to brace myself."

At this point, I would have loved to have seen a video of myself. I am sort of doing a handstand. And I would move my right hand real fast and hit myself in the naval, where the seat belt button is, and immediately move it back to catch myself in a handstand. I did this five or six times trying to undo the seat belt, and then catch myself by instantly moving the right hand back up into the handstand position. Nope. My antics didn't work. My tummy now hurts, but I still couldn't undo the buckle. Back to my thoughts, as I'm streaming profanities: "Okay, brace with left, press with right, and hopefully the left will slow me down enough it won't hurt as I fall on my head. Hard with the right. Really hard ..." *Click*....

What happened next? Nothing. I didn't move an inch. I undid the buckle, but I didn't budge. There isn't a whole lot of head room to begin with. And pressing with my legs as we rolled and I was bracing myself, I had my head against the roof. I am in the driver's seat, and my knees are stuck, wedged beneath the steering wheel. So I unclicked myself, and didn't move at all. Now I feel ripped off because I didn't get the full experience by being in the driver's seat. So, I am still hanging upside down, lodged between the steering wheel and the roof, suspended upside down, and I have to wiggle to free myself and crawl out. And you do get a little disoriented. You rarely get the opportunity to crawl out of an upside-down vehicle. And they shake you up a little and spin you around getting you a little dizzy ahead of time. It was different. But I untangled myself from the seat belt, and tried to open my door. It wouldn't open. The cadre can do that. To simulate the real world, they will only have one or two doors that will work. Mine wasn't one of them. So I crawled to the middle of the vehicle, and I see my front seat passenger, and she is still dangling upside down. She can't get her seat belt either. And she is this tiny little thing, so she had *a ways* to drop on her head. As I see her, she has both hands on the buckle, not even attempting to brace herself. If it released, she'd be hurting. So I called to her to stop her, and I look in the back seat. No one is there. The two back passengers both got right out and exited the vehicle. "Thanks for helping your buddies!" So I went over to the soldier who is still suspended upside down. I told her I was going to lean into her legs near her waist with my shoulder to support her weight, and press up to release the pressure on the seat belt. As I did this, she undid the buckle and then reached out and grabbed me. All this while upside down, in a vehicle upside down, in the area the size of a front seat compartment. It was cramped. But we got her freed from the seat belt, got her situated right side up in the upside down vehicle, and we both crawled into the back seat compartment and out the door. Success!

That was the first practical exercise. We had our little AAR (After Action Report) where we talked about what happened, and what went well, and what didn't go so well. We talked about how we need to help each other, unlike the two in the back who got free and escaped right away. And we climbed back in for the second endeavor. We spun around again very slowly, though it seems much faster when you are actually inside, and that stupid fire extinguisher keeps falling out of the sky hitting you, and a little rubber coke bottle keeps pelting you repeatedly. The instructors think it is hilarious to have all these rubberized items in the compartment rolling around with us. It is a little sadistic if you think about it. How many times have you wanted to put, say, a cat in the drier and turn it on? (I saw it in a Far Side comic.) Well, we are the cats. We climb in the little hole, get strapped in, and then the sadistic cadre close the door and turn it on, and giggle their little asses off as the ten little rubberized objects roll around inside hitting people. I didn't tell you, but there are microphones inside, so the instructors can hear you. There are also cameras inside, so they are watching you too. They think it is the funniest thing in the world. I'd love to throw them in, lock the hatches, and then find the speed control and see how fast we could spin them. But I digress....

Attempt number two had us land on our side. Unfortunately, it landed on the passenger side, so as the driver, I am dangling again up in the air. I am not upside down this time, but I am not right side up either. However, with the Humvee on its side, there isn't a good way to brace yourself to prevent yourself from free falling across the width of the vehicle when the seat belt releases. The width of a Humvee is a tad over seven feet. If you could spin your legs around just a little, that might work, but that isn't happening while still strapped in. Reaching down, my arms won't reach anything to help me brace myself either. What if I use my arms to hang on to something above me, kinda' like a sideways pull-up, to at least slow down my momentum as I start to fall? That might work. So I am fidgeting around, trying to figure out what will work, and I see the little pint-sized lady who was in the front passenger seat. She is out of the seat belt and crawling through the hatch. She was free... and she was gone! I squirmed a little more, got one leg wrapped around the steering wheel, and my right hand on a brace that runs along the roof, pushed myself up to release the pressure on the seat belt, undid the belt and climbed down. I looked in the backseat, the guy on the bottom was in the same place as the lady in the front seat, who was out of the hatch and long gone. But I had a full-bird colonel who was on the driver's side back seat who was still dangling. Since the Humvee was on its side, I was able to stand up this time at least. I did the same thing that I did last time which seemed to work, I put my shoulder into his waist and pushed him up a little so he could undo the seat belt, and then lower him down. Teamwork. It is the only way to go.

That was our experience with the rollover training at Fort Lewis. However, when we got to Kuwait, we had to do it all over again, because they have MRAPS (Mine Resistant Ambush Protected Vehicles). MRAPs are much bigger than Humvees. So we had to do the same scenarios. I was up front in the passenger seat this time. The MRAP simulator in Kuwait seemed to rotate much faster than the Humvee simulator at Fort Lewis. We landed upside down first. Not a problem. The last time, my head was resting on the roof. Not this time. It was a good foot and a half, maybe two feet from the roof. So I braced myself the best I could, and struggled to undo the seat belt. The next three sounds were *"click" "boom"* and *"boom"*.

The click is obvious. It is the seat belt coming undone. However, the seat belt was tight enough with all the weight hanging off it that I couldn't undo it with just the left hand. And as I tried to do it with just the right hand, I thought I was prepared to catch myself with my left hand. I wasn't. Where last time I was wedged in the steering wheel, this time, I wasn't. And last time I was concerned I was not strong enough with my left hand/arm to hold up about 300 pounds. My concern was justified. I wasn't. But why two booms? Well, I am assuming that as you read this, you are sitting in a chair. If not, imagine yourself sitting up straight in a chair. Now imagine that chair is suspended upside down, and you are magically sitting in it, dangling from the ceiling, defying gravity. Now imagine the law of gravity suddenly kicks in. As you plummet towards earth, your head is the first thing that is going to hit. Boom number one was my head hitting the roof, with 300 pounds of *umph* behind it. However, gravity wasn't done with me yet. Just because the metal roof of the MRAP was kind enough to stop my head, my legs and torso were still in motion. My torso started to bend, similar to a sit-up position. My legs continued with their momentum, and went from being bent, to starting to straighten out until their sudden impact with the dashboard. Boom number two.

Am I done? Hardly. I am now in an inverted fetal position, with 300 pounds of weight still on my head contorting my neck, and I have two bloody shins semi-permanently imbedded in the dashboard. Know how cars have padded dashboards for protection? MRAPs don't. I am a little disoriented from spinning around in the simulator, and I am a little bit stunned from getting my bell rung being dropped on my head. I told you it was about a foot and a half from my head to the roof of the MRAP. Defying all laws of physics, I felt like I dropped a good five feet onto my head. I now had to find a way to get out of the inverted fetal position with the contorted neck. I think I wilted, or drooped, something, over onto my side. I tried to get my bearings, but I am dazed and woozy in a topsy-turvy world of an upside-down Army vehicle. I wonder if this is what LSD feels like. I'm seeing double of everything, it's all blurry and spinning ever so slowly, with a few stars sprinkled in, and everything was upside down. In my trippy little world, I could tell that others were still dangling in the backseat. So, I stood up a little shakily, and instinctively went and put my shoulder into their waist to help brace them so they could come down. They came down all right, right on top of me. I could barely hold myself up at that point. What made me think I could support another 200-300 pounds? I couldn't. I crumbled under their weight, but luckily I cushioned their fall. They walked out fine. Well, as fine as you can walk out of an upside-down vehicle. Me? I am now the only person remaining in the vehicle, I am lying in a clump, and my new focus now is doing everything in my power not to puke. At some point, someone, I have no idea who—could have been an instructor, could have been one of the people in the vehicle to begin with, could have been Mickey Mouse for all I knew at that point—came in and lent a hand, and helped me wobble out of the vehicle. Come to think of it, I don't think it was Mickey Mouse. If it were a big padded white glove reaching out to help me, I like to think that I would have noticed. Maybe.

We did an AAR. I have no idea what was said, but I know we did one. We always do one. I was a little bit out of it. Can you say "discombobulated?" Someone said I didn't look too good. My head was pounding, and I just kept telling myself over and over again, "Don't throw up! Don't throw up! Don't throw up!" I don't think I tossed my cookies. If I had, I am sure that someone or lots of *someones* would be kind enough to remind me of it constantly. Then we climbed back into the MRAP simulator, and did it again, sideways this time I am presuming. But I am only presuming at this point. I honestly have no recollection. And then we were done. There are certain points in your life where you feel old. After the MRAP rollover training, I felt old.

Bin Laden

John Steele

This piece was written over the course of the first week of May, 2001, while stationed in Iraq.

On Monday morning, I awoke to the news that Osama bin Laden had been killed in Pakistan. When I saw it on TV, I was actually trying to check sports scores on ESPN, and they had something scrolling across the bottom of the screen that the president was about to make the announcement. So I flipped channels to CNN, and they were showing college kids from George Washington University assembling outside the White House. Then President Obama spoke saying bin Laden was killed. My first thought was "finally." Second thought was I wished we had him alive, get as much information from him as we could, and put him on trial. Third thought was reminding myself to be ever vigilant and safe, and I went to work.

Once at work, we passed on the information that he was dead. We told each other to be careful, and always have a battle buddy. We stressed situational awareness because that is what we do, but it has heightened with the events of the day. But that was the only real difference that we had here.

That night, I was at the gym working out in front of the television, and I was surprised at what I was seeing. The crowd outside the White House, comprised largely of students from George Washington University, was waving flags and singing. All across America, there were parties in the streets. At sporting events, people were chanting, "USA! USA! USA!"

I don't understand all the celebrating. The mood is very different over here. No celebrating. No flag waving. No high fives or chest thumping. No National Anthem singing. A hint of a smile, maybe a slight bounce in your step. And then, "Where is my vest, my helmet, and my weapon?" We expect reprisals. Some idiot in Florida burns the Quran, we get shelled a few nights in a row. It is announced that the U.S. military will keep some troops past the first of the year, we get nine mortar rounds in the middle of the day. (It was the only time since I have been here we have been shelled in the middle of the day. The most mortars we have ever gotten in one attack is four or five, and the most that have ever landed on the base is three. That day we got nine within a minute. It got our attention.) So when it is announced that we took out bin Laden, we fully expect some form of retaliation.

I have been having a hard time wrapping my arms around everything that keeps showing up on my TV screen. I have so many questions. The threat level has jumped here. There are intelligence reports that there will be increased attacks, and the targets will be U.S. personnel compared to the Iraqi forces. Why are people partying? I wonder how different it would be if I were home. Would I be partying?

I keep going back to the George Washington University students outside the White House. CNN reported that hundreds of these college students reveled all through the night chanting "USA! USA!" and singing "Hey, hey, hey, goodbye!" When they showed these students on television, half of them had beer in their hands. This is a mass murderer we are talking about here, not the rival to your favorite sports team. The typical college student is 18-21 years old. That would make them somewhere around 8-11 years old when 9/11 happened, a year younger when al-Qaeda attacked the USS Cole, and only 5-8 years old when al-Qaeda bombed U.S.

Iraq, Afghanistan, Other Places

embassies in Africa. Do they understand the gravity of the situation? The way the scene outside the White House is described sounds flippant. CNN described it as, "pure jubilation." This man masterminded the attacks that killed nearly 3000 Americans on 9/11 alone. He orchestrated numerous attacks all over the world, targeting civilians. How many families did he destroy? Am I glad he is gone? Absolutely! Celebrate? No. No way. The response should be more good riddance. A vile excuse for a human has been exterminated. Let's move on.

More questions: Bin Laden was found in Pakistan, in an affluent part of Pakistan, in a multi-million-dollar compound, ten times bigger than any other house around. Really? Not in a cave, or a hole in the ground? I saw the hole Saddam Hussein resided in, and I assumed/hoped that bin Laden had similar accommodations. No, he is hiding in a mansion in a suburb in Pakistan, 30 miles from their capital city, in the town that holds two Pakistani regiments, and their military academy, their equivalent of West Point, a half mile away. How could the government of Pakistan and their military not have known he was there? There should be a lot of questions for Pakistan. We have sent billions of dollars in aid to Pakistan since 9/11 for their assistance in fighting terrorism. Have they helped fight terrorism, or provide safe harbor for fugitives? If, like they claim, they truly didn't know, should we still be giving millions of dollars each year to a country that is that incompetent?

I saw Thursday that Pakistan warned the United States that if it conducted another unilateral attack within Pakistan, it would have "disastrous consequences." Again, mixed feelings. Part of me says, "Bring it on!" Then again, our military did fly into another country on two tricked out helicopters, shot up a house killing five, stole the body of one of them, and flew out. And on the way out called the Pakistani government and said,

"Hey, guess what we just did...." What would we do if some other country did that to us? We wouldn't be happy. If Pakistan isn't happy, we can cut off the over ten million dollars a year in aid to them. If we could trust their administration, were certain that they would not provide refuge, and knew they would cooperate, maybe we could have told them. Sorry Pakistan.

How the U.S. government got the intelligence on bin Laden's whereabouts is a mystery, as it should be. The media and the American people do not need to know. Not that it should go unchecked. Select government officials should be charged with monitoring the gathering of information, and ensure it is within regulatory guidelines. The media has brought up the possibility that some of the information on bin Laden's whereabouts was brought about as a result of enhanced interrogation techniques performed on detainees down at Guantanamo Bay, namely water boarding. It should not be allowed. (And if it is done, no one needs to know.) I don't care how much info can be obtained. Doing it to others makes it difficult for our government to object when it is done to Americans. I know that many of the terrorist organizations have no problem doing it to Americans. Doing it back doesn't make it right. We pride ourselves as being the greatest country in the world. Hold yourself to a higher standard.

When President Obama took office, he said that getting bin Laden "dead or alive" was a priority. Well, I would have much preferred alive. I don't know how much of an option that was. And we will never know. It has been reported that bin Laden's body was wrapped in a white sheet and buried at sea in a Muslim ceremony. I don't know how I feel about that. There is no grave site that the Crazies can go to and turn it into a shrine. So that is a good thing. Did he need an Islamic ceremony? I don't know. He didn't follow the teachings of the

Quran as interpreted by the majority of Muslims. He didn't care when he killed so many innocent people, including women, children and fellow Muslims. (Do you know he has orchestrated attacks in Egypt, Algeria, and Aden too? All Muslim countries) I personally would have been happy if they got the DNA and whatever evidence they needed, and then dumped his body in the ocean as unceremoniously as possible, preferably in a shark infested area. Hungry sharks. Or crocodiles. As long as there was nothing left. However, if that was done, many people worldwide would have had an issue, Muslim and non-Muslim alike, as would many Americans. So it is probably best they did what they did.

Another huge debate is whether the pictures of bin Laden should be published. No. Definitely not. The United States military is going to great lengths to strengthen the ties with people of the Middle East. What good will come out of showing the pictures? To gratify some Americans' morbid sense of curiosity? He has been caught, and is killed. That is all you need to know. Circulating pictures of bin Laden will only further alienate the United States with some allies in the Middle East, and more importantly with the population of those countries. U.S. service members are the ones who will suffer the consequences if those photos are released. Everyone who wants to see these pictures should be put on a plane, and send them to Iraq or Afghanistan. Then once the pictures are released, they can then spend the next year patrolling Afghanistan or the streets of Baghdad. What? That's too dangerous? That's crazy? You'll be a target? No shit.

Let's talk analysis. And this is not just on the television. A question that has been raised is, "Was catching bin Laden good for Obama, and will it win him re-election?" Do we need to pull politics into this already? I got something on Facebook Wednesday morning from a buddy of mine serving over here that said something to the effect that Obama didn't catch bin Laden, an American soldier did. (I didn't have the heart to tell him that it wasn't a soldier, it was a Navy Seal who got bin Laden.) This was less than 48 hours after the news broke. The meat off of bin Laden's bones hasn't even been digested yet by the sharks and crocodiles. Can't our country as a whole enjoy this little victory for a few days? Do we have to analyze everything, and come up with a winner and a loser politically for this? As you can guess, CNN and the non-cable networks all say it was huge win for Obama, and Fox News and most of talk radio say this is a win for the American people, and Obama had nothing to do with it. I hate to say this, but I am leaning towards agreeing with Fox News. (I hate agreeing with any of the news outlets. They all have a spin on things. Remember when news agencies reported the news? Just facts, no spin? I miss those days. Anyways....) Obama wanted bin Laden caught; as did Bush; as did Clinton; as did almost every American. Prior to 9/11, President Clinton wanted the CIA to bring in bin Laden to stand trial for the bombings of the U.S. embassies in Africa, and if getting him alive was not possible, than deadly force was authorized. Obama was on watch when bin Laden was caught, so he should get some credit. But if Mickey Mouse were on watch, bin Laden still would have been caught. It was the intelligence community and the military more than the President of the United States. In my opinion, what Obama did with the rest of the Global War on Terror, and what happened domestically would have a bigger impact on whether Obama gets re-elected.

Finally, did anyone hear what the code name for this operation was? It was called, "Geronimo." And Native Americans are not happy about it. I have to say that I agree with them. Of all the things they could have called it.... My personal favorite would have been Operation Goat-Fucking

Towel Head, but that would have been inappropriate too. Name it after an animal. Name it after an inanimate object. Call it anything you want. And they do. Operation New Dawn, does anyone know what that is all about? Does anyone even know that I am currently mobilized in support of Operation New Dawn? We are no longer in Operation Iraqi Freedom. In 1991 during the Persian Gulf War, it was called Operation Desert Shield, then Operation Desert Storm, and then Operation Southern/Northern Watch, all within the year. The development of the atomic bomb was called the Manhattan Project. The invasion of Normandy during WWII was called Operation Overlord. My point is you can call it anything you want. Why insult a portion of the American population naming it after one of their heroes. It was in poor taste.

I told you that the threat level was increased here at Victory Base Complex. But so far, it has not resulted in anything. Al-Qaeda has vowed to avenge bin Laden's death. However, al-Qaeda has next to nothing left as far as a footprint in Iraq. I think that most Iraqis are happy that the Saddam regime has been removed, and al-Qaeda has left to fight in Afghanistan. But it doesn't mean that there aren't some whack jobs out there still. Immediately after bin Laden was apprehended, our threat level went up. We get frequent intelligence reports, and all signs point to retaliation as al-Qaeda avenges his death. As a result, U.S. countermeasures have increased accordingly. The unit has had extra precautions that we need to adhere to. The threat of reprisal has affected our routines, especially at night. There are a lot less people out and about. A few weeks ago, I would head to the gym at 0300 to watch the Sabres (hockey team), and there would be people out and about. Since the Sabres have been knocked out of the playoffs, I usually hit the gym in the evenings, 2100 or 2200. Normally there are nearly as many people out then as there are in the middle of the day, probably because of the heat. But not this week. You feel safer in numbers, and there are no numbers out there right now. People want to get to their CHU's (Compartmentalized Housing Unit) before it is totally dark out, and then they don't want to leave. The last few nights, I have headed to the bathroom after dark but before midnight, and it is like a ghost town. It is eerie how quiet it is. You go to your CHU, and you try to sleep while at the same time listening for the big voice saying, "Incoming! Incoming! Incoming!" You listen for the C-RAM (Counter Rocket, Artillery, and Mortar), and to the sporadic gun fire. You lie there, expecting something to happen, and wait for daylight. Once daylight comes, and nothing happened, you figure it must be coming the following night. And then the next night. And then the next. It used to bother me when the mortars exploded and it would keep me awake. Now the mortars are not exploding, and it is keeping me awake. You can't win sometimes.

I just read the latest intelligence report. The name they have for it is funny. They call it, "The Daily Pessimist." Anyway, the vengeance they expected in response to bin Laden hasn't happened in our area. The threat level is remaining elevated for the time being, but as more time passes, the expectation of retribution diminishes. I am taking it as a good sign. I feel better knowing they think the worst is over, especially since the worst so far has been a few false alarms. Yeah!

Terry Jones

John Steele

It was a sunny day today, and hot. We were standing out on the runway in two small formations facing each other. The temperature was well into the 90's. It was windy, very windy, but it was of little reprieve. It was just hot air in our faces, blowing sand around. We stood there, waiting patiently. Not a word was said. No comments. No complaining. Not even a huff or a sigh. You could have heard a pin drop. Total silence except for the hot air blowing around, and an occasional couple of helicopters, or a plane taking off or landing. Before the formation, there was some fidgeting, and some hushed small talk, along with a lot of pacing. An abundance of nervous energy. But once in the formations, we were a bunch of little statues, other than wiping sand from our eyes here and there. The discipline: No one moved, no one made a peep. We stood like that for close to an hour, almost afraid to flinch. Anything less would be disrespectful. We were the lucky ones. Last night, a rocket hit Kalsu, a base a little south of Baghdad. 2 KIA, 11 injured, all Americans. We all stood there for close to an hour in the heat and the sun, just for the opportunity to render a salute for a few seconds.

As we were standing in the formations, a truck or some type of vehicle pulled up with the two coffins. I never turned to look to see for sure what it was. Eyes were straight ahead. A detail took the first flag-draped coffin, and very slowly and ceremoniously marched past the formations and up the ramp into the belly of the plane. Then the second coffin. After both remains were on the plane, everyone who was in the formations huddled around the back of the plane and said a prayer. Then everyone formed up in two lines and two at a time walked up the back ramp of the C-130. You march up to the coffin, slowly salute, (3 seconds up, 3 seconds down) do an about face, and march back down the ramp. Then the next two, and the next two....

Perhaps the hardest thing for me was later at the office. I was doing DTAS (Deployed Theater Accountability System), and I saw the numbers reduced by two. The numbers change up and down every day as a result of RNR (Rest & Recuperation), TDY (Temporary Duty), EML (Emergency Leave), MEDEVAC (Medical Evacuation) or RED MC (Redeployed Mission Complete). It was the first time I had seen a KIA (Killed In Action). We also had their Bronze Stars and Purple Hearts come through our office.

I'd like to think that it was just random violence, but it wasn't. It was a direct result of that pastor from Florida burning the Quran. It was well publicized that there were twelve victims at the UN in Afghanistan during protests. There were lots of protests here in Iraq too. They protested here around the US bases, since it was a U.S. pastor who caused the uproar. And they lob in indirect fire at us. For the past several months, most attacks around Baghdad focus on the Iraqi forces. A much smaller percentage target the U.S. soldiers. But I couldn't count the number of recalls we've done the past two days after it came out in the press that Terry Jones put the Quran on trial, found it guilty, and burned it. And it cost these two soldiers their lives. They will never see their wives again. They will never get to play with their children again. Both of them pre-deceased their parents. And why? So some wacko can have his fifteen minutes of fame?

The U.S. government tracks all of the extremist groups and organizations all over the world. The largest percentage of these groups in the United States are white supremacist groups that have "Christian" somewhere in their name. How offended would we be if someone did a mock trial and ceremoniously burned the Bible? Then multiply it exponentially for Muslims in the Middle East. Religion is not paramount in our culture anymore. For Muslims, their entire world revolves around Islam. The Quran is considered so sacred, much more so than Christians regard the Bible. That is their culture. And we know that. Or we should know that. The majority of Muslims are very peaceful people. Most of the Iraqi people refer to the radical Muslims much like we consider the skinheads who target Jews and African Americans in the name of Christianity. The radical Muslims are no more representative of Islam than the Aryan Nation or Christian Identity are to Christianity. Do we haul off and attack anyone with a Bible? No. And targeting the Quran is the same thing. Terry Jones' actions have consequences, and two families are mourning the loss of their soldiers. I'd like to put Terry Jones on trial here. He would be found guilty. And there is a whole brigade of soldiers here with weapons and ammunition who would gladly line up to partake in the firing squad.

BP Cuff

John Steele

Can you die of boredom? Absolutely!

We had an FTX (field training exercise). Two low ranking soldiers doing "guard duty" for hours on end in the middle of nowhere, with no one anywhere around. There was a trailer, empty except for a single box. A humongous three-foot deep, two-foot wide, four-foot long company first aid kit was our only means of entertainment. You can only play with so many band-aids, smell all the ointments, wrap up and pretend you're a mummy with the formerly sterilized gauze and ace bandages, and listen to various bodily functions with a stethoscope. Lo and behold, my buddy Ed discovers the blood pressure cuff.

"Dude, you can get so high by putting this around your neck. You limit the oxygen to your head 'til you get a head rush. It is so cool." So he put it on himself, pumped it up some. A few seconds later he released it and bragged how cool it was. I'm like, "Really?" I was never big on getting high, nor trying to choke myself with medical instruments. I'm sitting there dumbfounded, wondering, "Huh?" He's like, "Dude, you gotta' try it." "How?" "You've never done this before?" My puzzled look confirmed my answer. "Well, I'll do it for ya'. I'll pump. You let me know when you feel it." Okay. So he starts pumping. "60... 70... Do you feel it?" Not really. "80... 90... Anything?" I don't think so. "100... 110... 120... Dude, I've never seen it get so high... 130 ... "

That's about all I remember. The rest is hearsay. At some point, I just fell over and started convulsing. Ed released the blood pressure cuff from my neck. The convulsions stopped, but now I wasn't moving. Ed starts freaking out. As you may have figured out, Ed wasn't a stellar soldier. Or stellar anything. At this point he's pretty sure he'd killed me. Obviously, he didn't. I can safely say that when they say your life flashes before your eyes, that really does happen. The high feeling, I never did get that. The hang-over feeling, that lasted days. Days.

Marine

Suzanne Dianetti

The alarm went off to mark the start of my day and days to come, but this day was different. Michael—a US Marine Corps captain, his artillery unit, the 2/10—was in Afghanistan, Helman Province

Life would be different. He was the first thing I thought of the moment I opened my eyes, and the last thing I thought of before my head hit the pillow.

I realized quickly how utterly unimportant so many things were in my life, in my days, in the months and months (years?) ahead.

Flashes of the little boy; little league uniforms and trophies, high school antics, the day he came home from high school with the story of a recruiter and how he could be the "best of the best" as a Marine.

We had a conversation that day and I made a promise—that he had to graduate college first—then, after college, if he decided he still wanted to be a Marine, I would support him 100 percent, that I'd stand alongside him no matter what. Then, the years at THE Ohio State University and my visit at the end of his sophomore year when he told me he had decided to graduate in 3 years…. "Why, M?" I asked. "Because I signed on the line. I'm going to be a Marine—an officer." He replied.

I kept my promise from that day to this and will continue to do so. I kept it all through training, really tough training. I kept it through Afghanistan and Iraq and Kuwait. He's truly one of the few and the proud, and I'm one of the few and the proud.

The days leading up to deployment were agonizing. We'd never been together those last few days, but were constantly in touch. Sometimes the truck has been sold, and the gear is packed, all is set, then the news that orders have changed and the date is pushed back, and sometimes again, and again, then one day, he's gone. The stop-start, I'm sure frustrating for him, was nothing short of agonizing.

I've adopted every talisman I can—my daughter too—out comes the St. Michael's medal with the Marine Corps Eagle, Globe and Anchor (EGA). I wear dog tags with his name, rank, and the quote: "While I breathe, I hope." I attach the tag silencer, and never take them off. I added a star tattoo to my wrist to mark his first salute. I added an open star when he left for Afghanistan and had it filled in as soon as he returned. I added another open star when he left for Iraq, and had it filled in when that tour ended in Kuwait. I reached for and touched each talisman, on my chest, on my arm throughout those long days and nights. Always on my mind—where is he today, tonight? Is he in harm's way? Did he eat today, did he sleep? Did he receive the dozens of pairs of socks I sent to the desert? Did he share them—I hope so. Maybe the WIFI connection will work today and I'll get a quick response to the email I sent—all good news, all positive, always. Will he respond to the silly text game we played while he was in high school just so I knew he was safe? I'd text "Marco," he'd respond "Polo." All was well. And I'd cry. So many tears.

Of course, people knew he was deployed, but I will never understand, even when meaning well, why people feel the need to come to me and ask if I'd heard that 17 Marines were shot in Afghanistan today. I stopped watching the news when Michael was away.

As I write this today, Michael is home—Camp Pendleton in California—now with the 1/11th, still blowing stuff up. He's in and out of the field, back and forth from 29 Palms Marine Corps Air Ground Combat Center. He's home, and hopefully safe, always on my mind, that incredible son, boy, man, Marine—one of the few and proud...both of us...so many of us...*Semper Fidelis*, Michael.... I am and will forever be faithful.

Wedding Plans

Suzanne Dianetti

It was the plan, I think, for a long time—Lindsay wanted her brother to give her away on her wedding day. It was perfect. Amazing.

Then Michael's orders came—Afghanistan. He'd leave the U.S. in April with a possible return date mid-November 2012. The wedding date…October 13.

Plan B—her father and I, long divorced, would give her away.

The Marine Corps, of course, moved the departure date a few times, but Michael was in-country with the 2/10 soon enough, too soon, and our hearts and minds were with him. Communication was sparse, and news was bleak during that period of time.

Meantime, the wedding plans were in full swing. At the time Lindsay and her soon-to-be husband, David, were living in Washington State. The wedding would be in Pennsylvania, close to where they met at college, and in the most beautiful outdoor location.

Images of what a day-in-the-life of my artillery-officer son could be looking like, mixed with a trip to New York City and the most beautiful wedding gown. The images of Michael, mixed with plans for centerpieces that would sit on the tables of the beautiful barn, and what bouquets of daisies would look like wrapped with ribbon covered in embroidered bees. The clock was ticking. While gathering pinecones for the tables, I was also purchasing and shipping loads of socks to Michael...white socks, red clay...not a great mix...so socks were a commodity.

The third week of September a miracle happened—Michael called. So, if he's calling, I thought, he's okay, right. Thankfully, gratefully, yes, he was okay and better than okay, the unit's mission would complete early. Michael would be home a week before the wedding. "Mom, do you think Lindsay would still like me to give her away?" If you've ever just had tears spontaneously fall from your eyes, you can only imagine that moment for me. Of course...call your sister. It wasn't long before the phone rang again and it was Lindsay—in tears. We cried not just because "perfect" was back on the wedding plan agenda, but because, obviously, there would be a joyous homecoming.

We piled into the car the day before the wedding, Michael and I. My dress, his dress uniform (she chose the blood stripe over the white pants).

The day prior to the wedding was all preparation of the site and it was going to be just beautiful with an outdoor ceremony and a lovely reception in the barn, now decorated with lights and candles seated in tree cookies hand-crafted by David. Pinecones, leaves, clay pots...and in the middle of all of it was Michael—only he carried all he'd seen in the prior months—arranging centerpieces and setting up the bar. Surreal, truly.

Then it was wedding day and Michael's and my hotel rooms were adjacent to one another. I was ready—dressed—wondering what my Marine was doing next door when the hotel phone rang. "Mom, I need some help." Okay. I knocked on the door and there he stood—99.9 percent ready to go, looking amazingly handsome in that incredibly stunning

United States Marine Corps dress uniform. One last touch, though...the collar. The collar on the uniform is a giant hook-and-eye clasp. Michael hadn't closed that clasp since before Afghanistan, and the problem now wasn't that it was too loose; the problem was there was no way he was going to get it closed. Definitely a problem.

"Okay, Mom, here's what we're going to do. You're going to hold the clasp tight. I'm going to lean back as far as I can and you're just going to clasp it. Got it?" Yeah, right..."Okay." And on three...mission accomplished, but how my son was going to breathe all day and all night I had absolutely no idea, but we were dressed and ready to go.

Now, if you've ever worn your collar too tight, you know that things only get worse when you sit, and we had some sitting to do in the car. We made it to the wedding site without incident so things were looking good. While I helped Lindsay to dress, Michael walked the wedding grounds making sure everything was set, white chairs lined up just so, waiting for the guests to arrive. He walked into the lodge where Lindsay and I were finishing up girl things...like pulling on her striped socks to slide into her Frye boots (yes it was boot day for both of us!), and we turned to look at that Marine of ours. Medals all in a row, collar clasped and crisp, the midnight blue wool coat just a perfect fit. That's when Michael said, "Mom. I need a favor." Of course, anything. He raised his leg and set his foot on a nearby chair. "Mom, can you tie my shoe?" There was NO way he was going to be able to bend over in that collar to tie his shoe! I laughed so hard. *We* laughed so hard. Deep in my soul I saw the same smile I'd seen so many years ago when he asked me the same question.

And it was time. The witnesses, friends and family, were all assembled, and down the aisle walked the most beautiful bride and her proud Marine. Her arm was linked in his—dreams were coming true and memories were being made and soon they reached the arbor arch and when asked, "Who gives this woman to this man?" I heard, "I do." Michael did.

The Incredible Mr. E.

Tim Hansen

Whenever I received a nod to head out into the hinterlands of Afghanistan with the RAT team—Resource Assistance Team—I immediately thought of the primary essential for all soldiers in the field—food. I then made a quick calculation of how many rations I would need to pack and then thought of how to rearrange my rucksack for the trip.

Boxes of MREs, or Meals-Ready-To-Eat, were always within reach at the Office of Military Cooperation-Afghanistan in Kabul and the key was to sift through the tan plastic bags of meals, pulling out the more appealing entrees like spaghetti and meatballs, tuna casserole, or the sloppy joe mix. The one option avoided by all was ham loaf. It always tasted like processed cardboard.

Some *Joes* have elevated dining out in the field to an art form—perhaps done out of a longing for home or maybe to preserve that one thread of civility. And, to watch them is almost entertaining in itself. The masters of the craft always seemed to be the NCOs or enlisted soldiers. Most officers on the other hand had no inkling of how to get the full use out of this unique ration.

The MRE is based on the fact that a young soldier burns about 4,200 calories per day, but consumes only 2,400. A team of nutritionists and engineers from Natick Labs in Massachusetts somehow found a way to pack 1,200 calories into this sealed ration—not much larger than the conventional lunch bag.

Soldiers in the field can extract two meals from one MRE and possibly three when components are shared among other soldiers during break times.

"Time for Mr. E, Sir," I would hear from a young NCO or specialist eyeing and waiting for me to fall into the trap of asking, "Who's he?"

Instead, I'd surprise them by pulling out a bag from my rucksack and replying, "Got him right here, and tonight is Prince Spaghetti night for me." Most of the younger soldiers stared at me blankly, having no idea of the Prince Spaghetti TV commercials from the '70s and the wide grin on my face at my private joke on them.

Another great convenience of the modern MRE is the flameless ration heater. It's an ingenious device consisting of a temperature resistant plastic pouch with a cardboard tray slipped inside it and beneath it a packed mixture of magnesium, iron and salt. Adding water to the packet fill line sets off an exothermic reaction, generating sufficient heat to boil water. The end products of this reaction, magnesium hydroxide and hydrogen pose no threat to the environment.

Amazingly, the generated heat will warm up an entrée within two to three minutes. This device is priceless, because a warm meal consumed amid the deprivation and hardships of the field immeasurably boosts a soldier's morale.

The package of Charms candy sealed in the condiments packet was not only a sugar boost but also a way to build rapport by sharing those pieces of hard candy with children in the village. It was a simple gesture of friendship not scripted by foreign policy.

I would always save the slice of cake in the green sealed pouch for breakfast. Maple walnut was the favorite and most avoided cherry pecan like the plague. The cake slices were moist and went well with a cup of instant coffee—provided there was time to heat some water.

When there was no time to stop and sleep was scarce, the Ranger biscuit was the desired field-expedient technique to use. It consisted of pouring the entire contents of the instant coffee into one's mouth, followed by the non-dairy creamer. Next, add a swig of water to dissolve and mix the contents within the mouth and then swallow. The effects of the Ranger biscuit are always immediate, and the body pulls itself from the yawns of sleep.

Dover

Tim Hansen

We lifted off just after midnight in a Black Hawk helicopter from the grassy field known as Greenleaf Point—just behind the National War College at Fort McNair. I looked down as we passed over the Navy Yard on the Anacostia River, and then headed north over the jet-black waters of the Chesapeake Bay to Dover Air Base in Delaware to receive the remains of three soldiers killed in action in Iraq.

Dover—the only port mortuary in the continental U.S.—is a 45-minute flight from Washington.

I was the acting aide-de-camp for the one-star from Army Public Affairs at the Pentagon who had Dover duty that week. Dover duty, as it was known, is actually the dignified transfer host officer for the fallen. I volunteered to go, but for the general officers, it is like staff duty managed by a roster known as a Dash-Six. Each branch of service—Army, Navy, Air Force, and Marines—routinely listed their senior officers for this duty.

I used to think this duty hung over them like the Sword of Damocles, always having to be ready to depart at whatever hour when the sword fell. Yet, this time-honored tradition of transfer of remains became sacred to me during my time at the Pentagon, sharpening my sense of loss and deepening my unspoken honor to stand before our war dead in one last embrace and final salute.

My role was very minor, primarily to carry a sleeve of unit coins to give to anyone the one-star deemed worthy of receiving as a small token of appreciation and to assist the general in consoling the families through their agony of grieving and loss. But for me, it was important that I went there to face the inconsolable sorrow of these families and their friends.

Who wants to meet a grieving family at three in the morning and try to provide whatever comfort you can over the loss of a son or daughter? Their chalice of tears is the bitter sacrifice of war and there are no words or death benefit that can bring any comfort. Though the one-star and I were complete strangers to these families, the weight of their sadness shifted onto our backs as well and remained with us long after we left Dover.

We waited only an hour after arriving at Dover Air Force Base before an airman informed us that the Evergreen International 747 had just touched down. "We'll head out to the aircraft in about 20 minutes," he said sharply.

I looked over at the general. "Sir, is there anything I can get you?"

"No thanks. I'm fine," he said as if interrupted from deep thought.

I watched from the flight line as the jet taxied off the runway and took its place beside a row of KC-10 tankers. I looked back through the terminal window and saw the general speaking with family members.

I read the short bios of the deceased—none were over 30.

The airman stepped in from the flight line and escorted us out to the van. We joined the Port Mortuary chaplain and the honor guard detail from Third U.S. Infantry. Not a word was spoken as the van pulled away slowly from the terminal.

I remember the stillness of that morning as we walked under the glare of floodlights toward the aircraft. I felt a heaviness as I climbed the steps of the ramp, trailing the general.

The ground crew had removed the cargo pallets, and I saw the three flag-draped metal transfer cases at the cargo door. The honor guard processed forward and broke into two columns, standing on either side of the fallen.

The process of the dignified transfer had begun.

The Port Mortuary chaplain came forward and stood before the remains. His pause seemed like an eternity and though I never knew any of these young soldiers, I felt something violently ripped from inside me.

The chaplain opened his Bible and started to read, *"Yea, though I walk through the valley of the shadow of death, I will fear no evil, for you are with me; thy rod and thy staff; they comfort me...."*

My mind drifted as I thought of their lives and the cost their families must now bear. The sadness bore down on me again and I could only look down at the three American flags as ice water dripped from the cases and pooled at the edge of the aircraft's bulkhead.

Then, I asked myself why these men had to die. Why them? Will their sacrifice be remembered at home? Why are we still in Iraq? Why not me?

In this tradition, soldiers, sailors, marines, airmen stand before their fallen to offer one final salute before they go back to their hometowns. Nowhere else are the war dead honored by fellow soldiers in such an intimate, private and quiet way.

The chaplain finished reading and the honor guard stepped forward to move the coffins out onto the K-loader.

The general and I walked back to the waiting van.

When we got back to the terminal, I asked the one-star if he wanted to give unit coins to any of the airmen who helped us that morning.

He shook his head *no*.

"But, sir, I thought that NCO handled the whole mission very well, watching over us and keeping us at the right place at the right times. As a token for our appreciation...."

"We're down to our last few coins," he replied. "We need to conserve what we have."

I was incredulous for a second. But then realized that we work at the Pentagon, accountable for even the unit coins we distribute. Still, tapping a fund should not be a problem. How can lack of funds hamper a moment like this?

Shovel Dance

Steve McAlpin

I deployed to Afghanistan in February, 2002, and began what was to become the most significant phase of my life. Sent to the main military base at Bagram ahead of many of the soldiers in my unit, I was to serve as the "10th Mountain Division liaison" between Coalition forces and the local population. I had never heard about a liaison officer being appointed so believe the position was relatively unprecedented. I was a problem solver and as such, had intimate contact with several local officials.

In April, I received a personal invitation from the most powerful of the local warlords, General BabaJaan, to attend the Annual Charikar Freedom Festival. Under the Taliban, festivals and public gatherings such as this were strictly forbidden, so the event promised to be a great release for the many Afghans who remembered it from years past.

I was among a contingent of 12 Coalition Soldiers. After arriving at what was presumably the town square, we were ushered to the best seating on a makeshift set of bleachers. Base Commander LTC Edward Dorman III was introduced as the group leader and received a warm round of applause from an estimated crowd of over two thousand people.

My immediate supervisors, 489th Civil Affairs Commander LTC Roland deSelusout and Detachment Commander MAJ Donald Assburn recommended that we pass on the invitation, but I think it was just because they were not invited. At this point in the war, females were still forbidden from public events so there was not a female in sight. Though this practice was rapidly changing around the major cities, it was still too early to really see any progress on this front.

The festival was like nothing I had ever even imagined. A prominent Mullah said a prayer thanking Allah for defeating the Taliban and bringing the Americans to help move their country into a prosperous future. The prayer was ended as each Afghan ran his hands over his faces in a single motion from forehead to chin to cleanse himself.

There were six speeches given by various dignitaries. When they had finished, the crowd was exposed to ancient traditions that have been forbidden for many years. There was a cock-fight—outlawed of course in the US, and in Afghanistan until that very moment. It was brutal to watch. Worse still was a series of bull fights the likes of which I have only read about in magazines and books.

Blood spilled as one bull, horns gouging, tried to push the other bull out of a ring drawn in the sand. I was disappointed in that I had only six shots left on my camera which I wasted during the opening ceremonies. I usually had an extra role of film in my camera case—but not this day. I asked around to some of my colleagues—but they all had newly popularized digital cameras. Perhaps it was my dedication to Eastman Kodak Company in my hometown of Rochester, New York that kept me committed to regular film. Anyway, I just committed the rest of the event to memory.

Near the end of the festivities, I spotted a kite flying in the distance. It was the very first kite I had seen during my tour. I knew kite flying was strictly forbidden under Taliban rule—but they had been defeated and it was time to celebrate. The kite must have been a half-mile away—but its significance struck me instantly as I pointed it out to the colleagues sitting nearest to me.... Kite flying had become one of Afghanistan's most competitive outdoor sporting traditions and symbolized the very essence of freedom. So witnessing this symbol on this particular day was absolutely striking.

The most amazing event if the celebration was what I will call the "Afghan Shovel Dance."

This last act of the celebration served to sacrifice and pray for rain and a good harvest. Most agricultural societies have some tradition or prayer for a prosperous yield, but I cannot imagine anything more dramatic than the Afghan Shovel Dance.

After a few moments of silence, an elderly man stepped from the crowd and made his way to the center of the circle. With him, he carried an unusual looking shovel. While the dimensions appeared standard for a long-handled shovel with a wooden handle and pointed metal blade, there was the addition of a wooden cross-member about a foot up the handle from the blade. This addition provided the digger with the ability to dig a deeper hole if necessary.

The ancient man was rail thin to the point where one could count every rib. A toothless smile rested above a dirty white beard that flowed to his bare chest. He wore only a pair of loose-fitting white pants that shrouded his body from hips to calves. Each muscle ripped to its full extent as he used the shovel to support a long series of hops into the air. Then it really got interesting.

Like a high school baton twirler, he single-handedly spun the shovel over his head at an unbelievable speed. Then, launching the shovel into the air, he caught it behind his back. He demonstrated unimaginable strength and agility as he juggled the implement around his body and between his legs while performing still more acrobatics.

After a ten-minute series of shovel-tosses into the air, the man tried to stick the shovel into the dry earth near one edge of the circle. The ground was too dry and rocky to secure the shovel, so it fell over while the man jumped and danced to the opposite side of the circle.

Upon reaching the edge, he lay face down on the ground and clenched both hands behind his back. I felt a rigid uneasiness as the man crawled like a snake across the dusty and stone-laden circle, finally reaching the shovel.

The crowd went wild with cheers of encouragement as the man stood with the shovel in hand. He seemed utterly unphased by the blood and mud that covered his torso and pants. The pain must have been excruciating. He smiled broadly and after a few more impressive twists and turns, he was absorbed into the raucous crowd.

A single speech concluded the ceremony as the local Mayor approached the podium, carrying a light brown burlap sack. After a few words and affirming roars from the crowd, he opened the bag and freed a dozen white doves into the air. Again, the crowd burst with enthusiasm. Between the kite, the activities, the dance, doves and speeches, a reassurance fell over the crowd that the peace they had longed for since the initial defeat of the Taliban was here to stay.

Postscript: That was the initial defeat of the Taliban. During the 2002 and 2003 preparation for war in Iraq, American and Coalition initiatives in Afghanistan took a backseat to the Iraq War. Thus, permanently losing credibility with the Afghan people.

But I Have Promises To Keep

Mary Finucane

On a vacation with my family, we rent three cottages on the same property. In Cottage Three go all the grown-ups without children. In Cottage Two go all the grownups with their children ages eight through teen. And into Cottage One, the big cottage, the main house, go all the grownups with their children, ages 0–7. The main house holds the most people, and the most Pack n' Play Cribs, bottles, pacifiers, blankies, Lego's, wet swim towels, and swim bubbles. Every morning, the adults are on their 4th cup of coffee by 6 am.

I am in Cottage Two. It is bliss. The children sleep in a bunk room. There are no night feedings, no night terrors, and no children woken by the cry of another.

This is the first time in my adult life that my family has vacationed, all of us, all at the same time. My four siblings, their spouses and children, my parents. It took immense planning around schedules and here we are. At a lake. In the mountains. Together.

On the third day, I run into town for marshmallows to have with our nightly campfire. When I return, there is a change in the air. I enter the main house, Cottage One, which is always where the action is. It is empty, cleared out, except for my brother. He is standing in the corner, a phone to his ear, leaning. This is the only corner on the entire property where the signal won't die. If you hold a certain position, and don't make any sudden movements, you may be able to keep a connection. He is in this corner. Where are the crawlers? The babies, and their grownups?

At Cottage Two, I am filled in by my sister: there was an accident at Jim's work.

In Cottage Two, she is whispering, but the details are sparse.

The night carries on: campfire, bedtime for kids, grownups back at the campfire. It is then that the details emerge.

At Eglin Air Force Base, where my brother had just done his monthly jump before meeting us in the mountains, two servicemen had done their jump.

Something happened.

They collided in air.

Both died.

One of the men had just renewed wedding vows with his wife of eight years. Adopted a teenager. Had three small children.

They leave early, and it is no small feat. From the Adirondack Mountains to Florida: Jim, his wife, who is 8 months pregnant, their 6-year-old, their 4-year-old, their 2-year-old. They load the minivan to make a very long drive for the sudden memorial services.

As they packed, the two girls, ages 6 and 4, discussed…

The 6-year-old, fighting tears: *Why do we have to go! We just got here! We never get to see our Rochester cousins! I don't want to.*

The 4-year-old, quietly: *Something happened at Daddy's work.*

6-year-old: *So!*

4-year-old: *We have to go be there to help.*

6-year-old: *Why do we always have to be the ones to help! Why can't another family help this time!*

Three weeks later, I talk with my brother. I ask about the two men, their families. That accident had been buried under a new one: green on blue, he tells me. In Afghanistan, on a U.S. base, two Afghans turn on U.S. soldiers and open fire. Two men die.

"Shitty August," my brother says.

I am reminded that even when a war has ended in my mind, in the mind of many U.S. civilians, in that crisp and defined place where things begin, have a middle, then end, that this is not so. It's never really *over*.

Beneath the Tree of Life

Michael John Lemke

Leaves restlessly fluttering, dancing below the broad base of the withered old elm tree

Beneath which a skinny boy quietly sitting, pondering things, how his future might be

An angry man sputtering, romancing his whirling rage, wanting nothing but to be free

A lonely broken soldier's heart, slowly throbbing his life away, as his tearful brown eyes could see:

I only want the sun to shine on those colors yet another day

I only dream like the boy in a boyishly innocent way

If you could tell me, I'd listen to any of your truth to me say

I would, after all these years, hold any unlikely judgment at bay;

The boy's only joy was hope.

The man's only relief was expression.

The soldier's only world was pain.

But they got their soul back, a force for which the universe had to bend!

For you see my friends, that a boy's hope will re-invent the world, a man's expression can become a freeing revolution founding a nation of newness, and a soldier's pain shared can make the world wise enough to demand peace and brotherhood for all.

Out of the Tomb of the Unknown Soldier

Michael John Lemke

I did all that I could to not get anyone else killed, but failed miserably

I hid those things I would from many and none, my soul paled considerably

Until I sailed into the oblivion past despair, the port of the saddened heart so tried

My unmarked trail, wake of tearful shards of obsidian, ever so scattered and dried

I realize I am only fearful, a bard with idioms, and one unheard who has died

To no surprise, myself fallen hard and opened wide, against all probability

Having become the entombed in the unknown soldier's memorial, dry bones

Deep in the underground darkness of my own head, that knife's dull edge needing honed

Wondering if this dangerous neighborhood, indeed, were better than lead

Until the other Light Ones came to my own shadow's place of lacking presence

Offering only the solemn task of honoring the present tense, a cut fence along the wire

Of my human being, all I could ask, with a monk's silent saying prayers of nothing

To honor the seeing, the quietness of the fallen, not the appalling pyre

The imploded shell of my tortured soul's very fire

Defused and released from its clutch on death's door handle

Confused with relief from the constant vigilance of an eternally lit candle

Instead of a fused belief of internal bleeding and martyr's sandals

Out of the tomb I rise up and walk into the life still waiting for me, to live?

A Fallen Warrior

Michael John Lemke

Regardless of what war you have fought, this is for all the brothers who need another to spark some hope after all the shifting winds and sandstorms of loss and pain. Or maybe it is for some sister who is of a "good mind," as my Chippewa friend says. Either way I will share this future-story at the lightening fire circle here.

> It was many moons after I had counted coup. My wounds were closing fast as the antelope ran with me again. I went on a vision-quest, seeking what I did not know I needed for my own healing, as much for the give-away I did see coming. The grandfathers told me to be patient for the spirit-helpers would come with answers. One night, or maybe it was the unexpected day spent with Brother Eagle, I had this vision:

Looking Deer Stands Far

She was a like a vision in the desert sun, when I saw her face I forgot my thirst, she stands behind a tree

Freed without decision my heart sang, I felt the smile in her burst somewhere deep inside of me

She noticed with a subtle glance this hunter's circling dance, but knew there would be no kill

Her presence and direct gaze stopped me in my tracks; I stood, for once, absolutely still

When she let me slowly walk up beside her and touch the life I felt through her softness

Then the taste of cool berries in the forest shade her kiss so deliberately deliciously gentle

I could smell the meadow flowers in her hair; I could see she listened to Great Spirit's wind-voices

I could tell she had seen the other ones fall to the cougar's lair, but she had made good choices

She had run free to stay safe, but did not live in fear or hiding place, she only waiting wise

Her intelligent eyes danced with the joy of her sister Hummingbird, the little one's rapid flight

Her stance was well-placed for she had listened to the rock people and many stories over time

Grounded like the Turtle Mother, I pressed against her and could not sway, but she stayed unafraid

Which only made this Frog Clan brother only want to steal her medicine, have her attentions paid

I would do anything to have her be the maiden, who inspired my inner drum to beat as it once did

A complete and powerful beat to the rhyme of life with no sorrows expected in the tomorrows

But hope instilled by a wife, my borrowed marrow breathed alive in a garden place of redemption

And I living in gratitude and service for the gift she was, delivered without the price of strife

Nor torn or sundered by war and the plagues of other men, just her river of acceptance, her pool of forgiving

Love, as he showed both of us how to make it all right, not an endless, sleepless, fitful night

She was a star somewhere in the night sky, a bright one, a clear one; for she was of a good mind, mine.

Alien-Nation

Michael John Lemke

My desert night is the coldest of the coldest dark nights, one you will probably have the privilege of not knowing

You who are not like I am; for I am the least chivalric of all the bard-like knights into history's bloody flowing

Yet that is why I will survive against your pathetic apathy, your amazingly resilient and blissful unawareness

My cold steel sword of truth will slice your delicate and ignorant throat as you sleep, creeping into your consciousness, like a quiet thief,

I will steadily steal your peace which you cling to so joyfully ignorant of my world, my daily nightmare swirling

The tornado between my ears with all its rushing fears and destructive winds of timeless stench and decay

For when I tell my story, it's gory, not full of glory, not the patriotic mess they've made in your own head

And when you don't listen you deprive yourself of an informed understanding of your own generational sin

Not just of places you have not been and things you had the privilege of not doing, which may be your undoing

But my very existence as a citizen-soldier sent by you to YOUR war, which you can cleanse yourself from daily with a simple change of a thought or a channel

Streaming into your TV at night are my ghost-brothers, my
Wolf Band of the Cheyenne, and they will not let go

Nor will the ones we have lost, those who paid the greatest
cost, the very ones nobody can even name any more there
have been so many already, and their widows and orphans

Who will be the wife of such a madman, the neighbor of the
soul tormented by Legion, the friend of such an ill body?
Who will care when we die in your streets and jails, impaled
with the truth you could not, would not see?

The veteran suffers like Job, and has days when he curses the
day he was born; yet strangely would do it all again, yes even
go back for relief from your world, and perhaps, you
and your oddly irrelevant reality.

FAST FORWARD FLASHBACK

Michael John Lemke

I don't like hospitals anymore, but the people there usually care

I've been in ICU in a tent in Tallil, and AirEvac'd out of there

Today I'm getting cut for something trivial, hardware removal

But I don't like the smells, the alcohol, the whole scene meets my disapproval

See, I can't get it out of my mind, all the guys I saw lying there

First on the ground all over Iraq, and then in the air, I just stared

I remember I kept thinking of the ones who didn't get home

I remember the crying, how much they must have felt so alone

I remember the Flight Nurse coming over to me to see my stare

She said, "It's OK Sergeant, you're getting the hell out of here"

I looked at her face and her arm around my shoulder, told her

"It will never be OK for those guys, and I'm scared for mine"

Smiling she said, "It's OK you old Sergeant, you've done your time"

That's when I started to cry, because inside I knew it would never be OK, not then, not to this very day

This day they take some screws and a plate out of my left leg

And I'll smell the smells, and see the needles, and my brothers

I will see the brothers with no arms and legs, wheeling around

I talk to all of them all the time, and they give me straight story

I walk with them and open the door, hold the elevator, and more

I think about that "Freedom Bird" out of a stinking shithole place

I think about that flight nurse, and the look on her pretty face

Then I go to a place of total gratitude, for the bed that's waiting

When I come out of the chop shop, get fed, and hear someone stating

Something about politics or the election, I just laugh kind of sick

For all that dumb stuff I have no affection, not for those pricks

I'd like to see a disabled veteran run this country from his chair

Or like another FDR, the last good man for the people we had up in there

Most of all, when I head down that hall on crutches to the door and my Army buddy's ride, I will be glad to get the fuck outside.

I know the measure of any man's life is what he brought to his fellows, what he gave without taking, his word without faking

So I know the time I have left on the planet, even with a limp, will be consigned to give back in any way I can, to those who bought my bed today, with their lives and their pain.

Death

Holly Katie

We are quite the familiar acquaintances,
Death and I.
I feel a closeness with the dead,
that I don't the living.
I don't fear death;
rather, stagnation.
Death is the only guarantor,
the only certainty.

We have danced together many times,
and frolicked and screamed at each other.
"Why am I still alive?!"
"Why are you so dead inside?"
Death replied.
Hopes that were never given
respiration in the first place,
and dreaded doubts that would not die.

I confided in you,
how I contemplated Suicide,
and it took you instead.

What a sardonic irony,
that I must be the one to survive.

Alas, though you've crossed to the other side,
Death and I walk hand in hand.

Death reminds me of what's important,
and in exchange,
I give the gift of letting go,
witnessing the final journey
from this plane
to whatever's next.
Most are afraid of this thin veneer, but I...
I do not like to waste my *good*byes

Medal of ExHonorAte

Holly Katie

There is no medal for surviving your past
Triumphantly, haphazardly overcoming succumbing
To the previous generation's successive impasse

No guns a-blazin' here
Nay, only stealth-work
Hostile spies' repetitive lies in my ears

Really, who wants to be king?
Only an empty role, puppet to be ployed
For subtle subterfuge to supply the Others' making

Memorial Cards

Holly Katie

Memorial cards are the substitute puzzle pieces to place in the shadow left by the hole of the actual person [who] died.

I, Too

Holly Katie

I begrudge writing about PTSD, because I'm tired of it. And overall, it's gotten much better, but once in a while, a scenario will hit that will bring it all flooding back:

I haven't been in a combat zone, but I have grown up surrounded by violence.

Windows weren't blown open, but they were broken open with concrete pieces as petty revenge from a drunken college kid.

We didn't have security checkpoints, but we did have something stolen off our back porch and a stranger walked in our back door.

I didn't take self-defense until 2013, but when surprised with a German Shepherd puppy in 2002, we were told the reason was because of the break-in rape that happened two houses down.

I haven't heard bombs go off, but loud music past nine at night was the harbinger to the drunken and idiotic violence that would come next.

No one walked around with guns, but murders happened a few blocks away.

Our school never had shooter training, but one day they monitored the kids leaving as one was driving around Brockport.

I've never been in a burning building, but the one in front of our house burned down.

I haven't been awoken by bombs or mortars, but I have by loud sounds and an unwelcome presence in my room.

I haven't been surrounded by them, but I have seen bodies on the ground, one alive, one dead.

I've never been a medic, but I have watched someone die.

I was never a POW, but I was a prisoner of my upbringing.

In self-defense, they never said you might have to fight off someone you know.

I didn't go through survival training, but I trained myself, physically and mentally, to survive.

I learned how to de-escalate situations, without weapons.

I may not have been drafted, but I certainly was not a volunteer.

Over It

Holly Katie

I don't get over it
I just learn to live with the hole
Whole → _hole

And the Fruit Rolled Away from the Crabapple Tree

Holly Katie

I am not at all proud to admit that this is my *third* attempt at writing these thoughts. Perhaps in what could be considered dogged arrogance, I almost always get my thoughts out the first time, with little self-editing. But this topic is difficult because I write knowing it will be read, and for once I fear criticism and/or judgment for its content. It involves a long-held dream, never to materialize or to be realized, like the news of the sudden death of a close friend killed by his own hands. This dream holds so much more than one individual, and takes on the history of language imbued with culture and patriotic, perhaps even nationalistic emotion, of millions of people.

There is no set date for when it started, but the first time I ever thought of the military was in high school, at least. I don't remember much about a conversation I was once having about college, except tossing around ideas of how to pay for it, when the idea of the ROTC was brought up. I didn't realize the full extent at the time of what "being in the military" would mean, ROTC or not. But immediately I insisted it be the Navy, most of my family having enlisted in said branch.

I reached out to service members who were in the Navy. In short, I inferred the appeal: *Don't*. I was once asked, with the subtle tact of an elephant in a library, if I would be okay with the possibility of killing people. At the time, I wasn't sure, but

I don't remember the idea having any sort of sudden crushing guilt, since the concept of military being a force to kill wasn't exactly *foreign,* per se. They, however, seemed convinced that I would, and they didn't seem to have any problem expressing it. My background of religious fundamentalism, which preferred boys instead of girls and desired masculine traits in women to some extent, also reinforced the idea that women don't belong in the military, along with the notion that they are "too emotional to lead." I also was taught that women were "too emotional to vote," but that's for another time.

Mind you, (though how would a reader merely know this?), that I was already primed for a militant mindset since age 5. My tiny world, a sub*cult*ure within a subculture, taught me that the world was dangerous, within and without the home, though I was not consciously aware of the over-activation of my sympathetic nervous system in high school, jumpy as I was at the slightest noise. Life was a never-ending Wonderland of chaos and unspoken land mines for rules. Not only was happiness the only emotion allowed, and any semblance of individuality not, but even the slightest quirk of my mouth in disagreement or nudge of my eyes indicating disdain would be called out and castigated. 'Personal boundaries' was not in the dictionary, and only 'propriety' in the sense of religious 'modesty,' aka in secular circles 'slut shaming.'

With the inner world already eradicating a sense of self before a sense could even be established, and the IOUs arrogated to us offspring to support the "family unit" even unto the expense of ourselves, my stoic interior turned itself instead to the outer world's terrors. I soon came to fear voices at night, knowing how to tell how drunk they were by their timbre and amplitude, wondering what the ratio was for level of inebriation to level of destruction. Thank god for telephone poles; both ours and our neighbor's house were saved from having drivers crash into them.

Without hailing a dirty laundry list of the events that took place outside, I certainly didn't take evening strolls once the sun set. It didn't help that I had been informed with grisly detail of multiple accounts of the methods of killers and kidnappers for luring in victims.

***

I didn't really think much about life after graduation; I've always been one for goals, but not realistic conceptualization. Life took an unexpected twist when my principal handed me a HESC scholarship for college, for which I had applied to exactly none. That May, on a whim, I visited MCC and decided to attend, wanting to study language, having already studied Japanese and taught myself to read Russian and Arabic. No language program available, I stuck with Liberal Arts. Due to my religious beliefs at the time, my militaristic focus began to shift to the IDF (Israel); I wanted to enlist with the Caracals, an all-female combat unit on the front. However, I also worried about my dysmenorrhea, being completely, excruciatingly disabled at least one day a month. The IDF said *no*, since I was neither converted, nor a citizen.

My thoughts about the world also began rapidly expanding, as one brave soul took the time to open up to me about his life in Iraq pre- and post-invasion. Beliefs about politics shifted as well, and at one point I had done a 180°, wanting to renounce American citizenship after learning what other countries thought about us. (When I was in Australia, I was rather closeted about the fact that I was American, though once I had gotten into deeper conversation with the strangers I'd met,

Iraq, Afghanistan, Other Places

only then would I reveal it, to which I was relieved that they were pleasantly surprised by how I presented myself).

I feel it's important to acknowledge that I wasn't anti-military; I was, and still am pro-peace. The military is a respectable job, but one that indeed is paid for with a life; they are the political garbagemen of the world, so to speak: it's a smelly job, but until the trash (harm and violence) learns how to take itself out (ceases to exist), someone's gotta' do it. And toward the end of 2018, I was contacted for the first time in years by a recruiter. Thinking I had quelled that desire long ago, it lit right up like white gas on a match. This time, I followed through with my desire to commit my life...

... to hear a *no*.

Buckle your seat belt, folks, the coaster is taking its plunge.

Half a year later, I'm coming to terms that I am still angry, and so very sad. I would have been damn good. Along with all that's previously written, I'll shove my premises here as to why the military missed out on leaving me behind: I can survive with a heavy pack into the middle of godforsaken nowhere, where the most advanced technology is a miniscule gas stove and a flashlight, and manna was a lean-to and privy; I scored *really high* on my ASVABs—a 96 out of 100, language being the highest (I received phone calls from recruiters, like telemarketers, to an unlisted number). I went from behind the pack in PE to leading the front running, earning the nickname, "THE BEAST"; I already didn't think as an individual, and could turn off the bodily signals of my needle reaching; even though born an empath, I could keep a stone face through some of the most emotionally rigorous moments, as needed.

The problem, not aforementioned, was a diagnostic acronym: BPD. The Air Force recruitment office informed me that I couldn't be on medication, either, which I had already tried to function without, merely a wee 5mg short-life amphetamine salt. Already having PTSD probably didn't help matters any either, though I'm hazy as to whether I mentioned that or not.

BPD, what I guess is a similar, if not the same reason, another family member also was rejected from the military. I don't know much behind the story of their enlistment, though. They were advised to not continue their military enlistment due to his family history. I, also a branch of that family tree, was turned down with a polite rebuff.

***

My hesitation and dilemma with writing this all out is for those who experienced the other end of the spectrum of having no choice, to which they were drafted. To even have these reveries, let alone speak of them, seems an egregious insult to those on the other side; every veteran I have shared my abiding desire with have all agreed: I'm better off for having not enlisted. I know they are all right, and it feels puerile to express that I wanted to find out for myself. The regret, hatred, experience, boredom, all of it, I wanted to learn for myself. While trying to join the IDF in my early college days, I explicitly spoke aloud to myself, "I want to go through it, because I want to understand what they go through." I never will, not in the way I wanted. It's not the same, but these are the experiences I *can* speak to:

- Writing letters to friends, since other forms of communication may be monitored or inaccessible

- Hiding in plain sight, even accidentally
- Holding my breath steadily, no matter how terrifying whatever's around the corner
- Staving off hunger, and other basic needs until safe(r)
- The possibility that a distant threat could show up at any minute and *fuck shit up damn quick*
- Thriving in chaos and emergencies
- Listless in the calm
- The vivid nightmares, and daytime flashbacks
- Hitting someone I love in self-defense
- Sudden bouts of rage, and bouts of The Void just as quickly
- Surviving suicidality and the desire to harm
- Not recognizing my reflection, photographs, or surroundings
- More gaps than memory
- The endlessness
- Creating my own "family" from experiences shared
- Innovative creativity
- Empathy
- The ability to lead
- Recognizing the signs of someone in crisis
- A sailor's mouth

- Me-search turned research
- An indomitable spirit

The Big Demon

Holly Katie

Trauma
An ugly demon
It requires space
Demands time
Drains energy

Why not just get rid of it, you say?
Well, biology, I reply
My body remembers what my brain cannot
My eyes are adjusting to the sunlight
Which I have never before seen
And something so good
Overpowers me

So I retreat to the cave
To rest from the shock
But back into the dankness
Which once my innocence took

Has left me destitute
And blinded eye
Something to OUTSIDErs
I can't describe

I burn easily
But crave the warmth
I fatigue from heat

Not knowing it's water I need

Never having been taught
In the cool dark caves
Yet survival expected
From land dwellers' ways

For they have not been in the depths
Nor raised in it
They get claustrophobic
And outside, I, lightheaded

Two worlds
Yet one
I spend my days
Dying in the sun

H-E-L+L-P

Holly Katie

Helping someone against their own will
Is one of the most twisting, mind-fucking emotions
You're helping them stay alive for their own good
Or so you tell yourself
It's like
The only way
To save you
Is to violate you
Invalidate your request
Invade your space
Break your trust
Embarrass you
"All for your own good,"
Because if I don't help you
And you die
I live with the guilt of not helping you
And perhaps you lived your last days
Thinking no one would reach out
And if I do help you
I then live with *that* guilt
So which guilt do I pick?
To help someone like you
Because whether I help
Or not
It's my fault

United in Service ★ United in Sacrifice

So let's rape both our consciences
-you feel guilty for asking-
-I feel guilty for responding-
To keep you alive
For god knows what reason
You're welcome

CONTRIBUTORS

Contributors

**Suzanne Dianetti**, joined the RVWG in 2019 as the mother of an active duty United States Marine Corps artillery officer. Michael, now a Major having just reached his 10th year of service, has seen two deployments: Afghanistan and Iraq, served at the Pentagon, and soon will be in Bahrain for two years. Suzanne is also a former USAF wife of a physician. The family served together from 1990-1994 at Laughlin AFB with the 47th Flying Training Wing in Del Rio, Texas. She has a Masters in Human Development from the University of Rochester, is certified by the DoD to teach yoga to Veterans through their Yoga Warriors protocol, and has taught yoga and meditation for over 20 years. Her daughter, Lindsay, resides with her family in Tacoma, Washington where she uses her dual masters for the State Department of Public Health. Currently Suzanne works with military veterans through a local nonprofit organization. Being part of the RVWG and a witness to these stories has been both an honor and privilege.

**Mary Finucane**, Mary Finucane co-founded RVWG with journalist and retired Lt. Col. US Army, Tim Hansen. She is incredibly grateful to have spent some of the finest Saturday mornings at Writers and Books, caffeinating and writing with members of RVWG. Finucane is daughter of a Veteran and sister of an Active Service Member. She will never know all the acronyms of the Armed Forces, but she is honored to bear witness to the stories that have poured forth from the pens and pencils of those who showed up and scribbled alongside her.

Tim Hansen is an Army veteran and cofounder of the Rochester Veterans' Writing Group. He has worked as a public affairs officer in Afghanistan, Kuwait, and the Pentagon, and now works as a technical writer for a medical device company in Rochester, New York.

Holly Katie wanted to serve in the Navy since high school, as many of her family had done before her. After graduating, she pursued her BA in Linguistics and is currently finishing her thesis for an MS in Human Development. While in graduate school, she was contacted by the Air Force for enlistment but soon found out she would not qualify because of her history of mental illness. Though disappointed, she sought the next-best option: working with veterans.

Through a series of bizarre coincidences, her work as a model landed her a job at a location where a contact of Tim Hansen's worked. Fast-forward to present-day, Holly is currently a part of the Rochester Veterans Writing Group. Though she was never able to serve, her hope is that with her experiences from exposure to abuse and violence, she can help narrow the gap between the civilian mindset and military by being open about her PTSD, amongst her other illnesses, and her haphazard journey through the healing process.

Contributors

Michael John Lemke was born in Chicago, IL, on February 24, 1959, joining the Army in 1977. Between 1977 and 2005, he served a total of 15 years between the Active Army, Army Reserve, and Colorado National Guard, including at a nuclear missile site in the Federal Republic of Germany. He graduated from SUNY Geneseo in 1984, majoring in political science and history. He worked in various teaching and military training, mental health and specialized counseling, and in transportation and law enforcement occupations. He deployed to Kuwait on, February 21, 2003, for the initial invasion of Iraq with the 220th Military Police Brigade, then medically evacuated from Tallil Airbase, Iraq, in 2003. He retired from the Army in February 2005 to Rochester, NY, where he enjoys his time with freelance writing and veterans' advocacy.

Steve McAlpin, US Army, Retired. 1978-2006. SSG to MAJ. Germany, Bosnia, Afghanistan. Served as a Carpentry/Masonry NCO, Combat Medical Specialist NCO, Infantry Officer, and Civil Affairs Officer. Enjoys writing, woodworking, painting, archeology, travel, and supporting veterans with whatever time and means I have.

Joseph Mele Jr. is on a mission. There's a story in the hundreds of letters that were found when his mom passed on  in 2012. The letters date back to 1934. Many of them are from the WWII years when Joe's father was the surgeon with the 749th Tank Battalion fighting through France, Belgium and Germany. It's become Joe's mission to provide background and context for the letters, and to tie them into a cohesive narrative.  Joe's retirement from software test engineering in August, 2018 allows him time to devote to writing. The Veterans Writing group provides insight into a soldier's experience, as well as camaraderie and healing.

 **Rori Murrell.** Three years—Women's Army Corps. 38+ years—Licensed CSW/ACSW and Certified PTSD Specialist, ongoing—Participation in various Veteran activities; available for hospice and pro-bono work with Veterans and their families.

Contributors

Janice Priester-Bradley. On April 1st, 1986, Janice challenged herself as a Registered Nurse and made a dual career by joining the United States Air Force. As a second lieutenant, her mission as a Flight Nurse, 69 A.F.B. N.J., as a member of the medical team was to accompany military patients from Germany to the U.S. and vice versa. Advancing in rank to first lieutenant, she was known for her teaching and leadership skills. Her first deployment was Desert Storm and Shield. Janice enjoys relating to people and she was recognized for her assertiveness. Therefore, was given the nickname "Princess P." After relocating to Rochester, N.Y., her new base, 174th Syracuse, N.Y., she was assigned as the base Cardiopulmonary Resuscitation Instructor (CPR). Her second deployment in Afghan-istan, ranked as captain, she maintained her stamina, when a General pointed his finger in her face and stated, "This is the highest you will ever go." Let go and let God. Janice kept her head up and stepped into a major rank, and became the 174th Base Health Promotions Officer. She continued this role until her third deployment, 911/New York City. Her 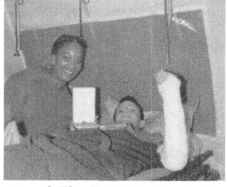 fourth deployment was devotional, The Haiti Mission. Janice states, "As I held this child in my arms and saw her crushed torso, I cried to the heavens to ask God to help me, so that I could help her." Ranked as lieutenant colonel until her retired date, she took on the role as the leader for the base-wide

Health Promotions Program at 914th Air Force Base in Niagara Falls, NY. She spearheaded this program and was awarded her last medal, the Meritorious Service Medal, which reflects a job well done. She remains a current charter member for the Women in Military Service Memorial in Washington, DC, as she retired on May 1st, 2014.

Gary Redlinski. After an education to pursue a career in funeral service as a director and embalmer, Gary Joined the U.S. Army in 1967 and trained for the Graves Registration MOS. From May of 1968 to July 1970, he served as an Identification Specialist at the Army Mortuary located on Tan Son Nhut Airbase, outside of Saigon (Ho Chi Minh City), Republic of South Vietnam. During his tour at the Mortuary, he handled and processed thousands of soldiers' remains. His writings reflect those memories of his experience as a soldier during that war.

Contributors

Sue Carmichael Spitulnik, was an Air Force wife from February 1972 to July 1979. She lived in multiple states and England during that time and had two children on "Uncle Sam's Nickel." She now resides in her home state of New York. She and her husband, Bob, count family dinner day the best day of each month. She is a member of the international writing group Carrot Ranch Literary and also belongs to Lilac City Rochester Writers group. She has been a participant of the Rochester Veteran's Writing Group since 2015. When she isn't creating with words, she creates with color in her quilting studio, specializing in patriotic and t-shirt quilts.

Vaughn Stelzenmuller writes to get people to read. His five-year military career piled up ample material to do just that. After commissioning into the Regular Army from Johns Hopkins University in 1967, the government posted him to Fort Hood, Texas; Central High-lands, Republic of Vietnam; and Stuttgart, Germany. He writes about what happened as an infantry officer, the sorts of things about which most veterans would chime in, "Me Also." Most of those things can be humorous, some less so. When veterans write, everybody learns. Vaughn made captain after two years' active service—which every officer did then, who refrained from getting sent to the stockade. After active duty Eastman

- 265 -

Kodak Company hired him as a manufacturing engineer. Now he writes. He is still working for "promotion to captain" in real life. It isn't easy.

Master Sergeant **John Steele** served in the Army and Army  Reserves from 1985 until his retirement in 2015. He entered the Army as a combat engineer, worked his way up to squad leader and platoon sergeant, and eventually worked in positions as an instructor and in administration. On the civilian side, Mr. Steele taught Special Education for eleven years, and after 9/11 worked for the Department of Defense for another decade. He started dabbling with writing in 2011 during a year-long tour in Iraq, and joined the Rochester Veterans' Writing Group in 2015.

 **Bob Whelan** started life as a rear rank infantry private, danced through 36 musicals, and wound up as a back-row tuba player. Not a great accomplishment, but it could have been worse.

Read all about it....

Contributors

Charles F. Willard. Chuck was brought up in a rural setting, tending the family's animal herds from the age of six. He attended Syracuse University, studying engineering and taking Air Force ROTC instead of gym. This led to a four year career as a pilot of C-130 Hercules aircraft, flying missions into 42 countries, including numerous operations in Viet Nam and Southeast Asia. In his subsequent engineering and management career at Xerox, Chuck had the privilege of leading the team that developed the world's first laser printer. Now retired, he spends his time enjoying family, golf, woodturning and writing. In addition to veteran's stories, he has three unpublished historical novels to his discredit. He deludes  himself that he could resume his old pilot's job at any time, since the US Air Force is still flying C-130's.

Prompts

Following are selections that you can use to form your own writing group. There are different types and styles to show the prompts can be connected to great books, movies, quotes, or just everyday happenings. Hopefully, the examples will be enough to get you started then you can also come up with your own, maybe more pertinent to where or the time you served. The formats are different, as they were written by many different veterans.

SELECTION 1

After finishing basic and training you receive your first orders. The moment you heard where you would be stationed or deployed...
- What did you tell yourself?
- What did you tell others? Who did you tell first; how and why?
- How did the reality of finally being able to use your training compare to what you expected?

When it was time to go home...
- During your deployment, what did you tell yourself it would feel like when you got the orders to go home? - How did the reality compare?
- How did you tell others/family?

Getting Home
- How far did you have to travel from - to where?
- What was the first thing you wanted to do?
- Who did you trust to tell how you were feeling, and in the aftermath, what was it really like for you? How did that person earn you trust? Are they still in your life?

Did you keep any souvenirs from where you were stationed? Did you purposely leave any possessions behind? If so, what and where?

If someone approaches you and asks if serving your country is a good or bad thing, what would you say and how would you guide them?

Selection 2

A. Prompt #1: Perception and Reality. Phil Klay writes about an Army vet who returned to school and found himself defending his actions to the assistant dean of student affairs at Amherst College. "'In the Army, we had a saying,' I said. "Perception is reality. In war, sometimes what matters isn't what's actually happening. The Southerners think Grant is winning Shiloh, so they break and run when he charges, and so he does, in fact, win. What you are doesn't matter ... You get treated as you're seen. Perception is reality." (Phil Klay, *Redeployment,* 2014) What was your perception of reality when you were on active duty? How has it changed since you returned home?

B. Prompt #2: Fatigue. Ernst Junger describes the weariness after a battle and the fatigue to get things done when he served during WW I." Exhausted by the strains of this momentous day, we settled down in our holes, except for the sentries. I pulled the ragged coat of my dead neighbor up over my head and fell into an unquiet slumber. Towards dawn, I woke up shivering, and discovered my situation was sorry indeed." (Ernst Junger, *Storm of Steel,* 1920.) Describe the fatigue you felt whether from combat, marching all day to the objective, or just a long day at work.

C. Prompt #3: Memory and Recall. "Memory is an inherently interesting thing. You think you know what it is, but when you think about it, you realize that you don't, " said Michael Bicks, writer and producer of the recent documentary M*emory Hack*s from the *PBS* series *Nova*. Writer Reed Tucker explains further: "Researchers have discovered that memory is changeable. The act of recalling something alters it. Forming memories actually causes a physical change in the brain... When you create a memory, new synaptic connections grow between neurons in the brain. But each time you call up a memory, it must then be resaved like a file on your computer — and it gets modified in the process. Dutch psychology professor Merel Kindt has seemingly found a way to erase the emotional anxiety associated with bad memories without erasing the memories themselves. Working with arachnophobes, she discovered that subjects who were given a drug called propranolol after being exposed to a spider were later able to handle the creatures without fear. The drug is believed to change the way a memory (in this case, terror associated with spiders) is resaved in the brain after being accessed..." Further research with the memory-altering drug show mice, once given it, do not freeze when placed in an environment in which their typical response would be to crouch and freeze. They just keep moving, exploring, and demonstrating behavior that shows an absence of fear.

If you could alter a memory, strip it of its emotion and hold it as a neutral recollection, would you? Why, or why not? How has a particular memory impacted your life? What hidden gifts has a memory of significant weight given to you?

Selection 3

My Unforgettable Person - For decades, Reader's Digest magazine has run a section titled "My Most Unforgettable Character". These stories usually describe teachers or mentors, friends, or even famous people the author has encountered. We've all known these people in the military, from gruff-but-fair platoon sergeants to by-the-book COs. But those people don't define our service. Those we served next to count much more. Tell us about someone you served with who is unforgettable. But make it someone who made your service more bearable, someone who had an unusual habit or personality, or someone you remember fondly, though, not that hard-case captain who conducted inspections every Saturday morning.

Stuff We Have - Almost all of us have one or more artifacts or souvenirs from our time in the service, or maybe even from another family member's service. Most of these are just stuff that we just happened to have in our possession when we were discharged or were handed down to us. As such, they bring up old memories when we encounter them but are not that significant. My father-in-law has three service buttons he took from captured German soldiers after the Battle of the Bulge. Holding them in my hand gives me a richer understanding of his efforts during the war. If you have some item of "stuff you feel is significant, tell us about it, how you came to have it, and what it means to you.

Chance or Choice? - From the day we enter the service there is an endless number of scenarios that can play out for us. All of us have encountered carefully executed plans, chance meetings, lucky (or unlucky) timing, and sheer dumb luck that shaped our service experience. In auto racing, there is a saying that "lucky is just that place where opportunity meets preparation". Some of the situations we encountered met this definition and in others, we had some measure of control. Describe an experience where there was more than one possible outcome and tell us how it happened, why you think the outcome occurred the way it did, and how it affected your service and/or your life.

Support the Troops – It's not hard to express support for our service members and veterans, be it volunteering to help with Honor Flights, a casual "Thank you for your service" comment on Veteran's Day, or a donation to organizations like the USO or Wounded Warriors. But almost all of these expressions occur after the fact or at best while our military is actively engaged somewhere. Not to belittle them, but are they the true bottom line for "supporting the troops"? Look deeper into what you think supporting the troops really does (or should) mean and express how you feel we can best make it happen.

SELECTION 4

A. Prompt #1: "Comfortably Numb." Chris Hedges wrote in *War Is a Force That Gives Us Meaning* (2002) that "one ingests war only to remain numb. The world outside war becomes, as Freud wrote, "uncanny." The familiar becomes strangely unfamiliar many who have been in war find this when they return home. The world we once understood and longed to return to stands before us as alien, strange, and beyond our grasp." In what way did war change the familiar to the unfamiliar when you returned home? How did you handle the unfamiliar?

B. Prompt #2: Team building or mind control? In *Band of Brothers* (1992), Stephen Ambrose wrote about soldiers learning unquestioning obedience and the consequence of violating orders. "The Army had a saying, Gordon related: "We can't make you do anything, but we can make you wish had.' Brought together by their misery, held together by cadence counts, singing, and common experiences, they were becoming a family." At one point after all of the training and discipline, did you feel that your unit or section became a team or a family?

C. Prompt #3: the Vietnam syndrome and spouse abuse. Catherine Lutz writes about a civilian family services worker at Ft. Bragg ripping apart New York Times and Newsweek articles that referenced higher rates of abuse in military families in her work, *Homefront* (2001). She wrote: "They drew, he said, from the myth that the military attracts or produces more violent people. That fiction was created by the Vietnam syndrome, the common term that describes certain views of war and interventionism as an illness." How do families adjust to long deployments and long days at the motor pool? How do military families live with sacrifice?

Selection 5

1. WOULDA, COULDA, SHOULDA – Everyone who has served had plans for their life BEFORE that service. Some may have actually started down their life's path when they were drafted or enlisted. Others may have considered a military career from the start. What did you envision for your life's path and where were you on it when you entered the service? Did being in the military affect that path? Did it help, hinder, redirect, or even change that path entirely? Tell us about your planned path and the one actually taken.

2. THE KIDS THESE DAYS... - I was four years out of high school before I started college.
When I graduated I wound up in a group of younger engineers, most of whom had never been personally exposed to military life and whose work ethic and priorities were somewhat different from mine. What is your perspective on the differences you have encountered between you and those who have not served? Don't dwell on the question of respect for your service (we've already dealt with that informally on several occasions), but tell us how you relate(d) to non-vets.

3. AH! NOW I REMEMBER! - In interviewing my father-in-law about his service in World War II, He kind of breezed through it in a couple of interviews. When I drafted his memoirs based on those interviews and let him review them, it jogged his memory about other, more personal experiences. As a result of those later recollections, the final version of his memoirs was more than double the size of the first draft. Describe some small personal aspect of your service that you just happened to recall one day and what brought it to mind. It doesn't have to be about something really important, just some small thing you remembered and want to share.

4. YOU GONNA EAT THAT? – Military food has probably been the subject of stories, jokes, and recollections, most of them unpleasant or at least disappointing, since a starving Continental Army soldier first dropped a possum into a cooking pot at Valley Forge. On the other hand, sometimes we were pleasantly surprised by the ingenuity and creativity of the military cooks. Tell us about your best (or worst) culinary experiences in the service.

5. THE PLAYING FIELDS OF WAR – It has been said that the traditions and success of the British military "began on the playing fields of Eton". Some aspects of sports and military action are often described in similar terms. In football we have "the blitz" and "the bomb"; a last-second move into a corner to pass a competitor is often called a "dive bomb" in auto racing. General Norman Schwarzkopf more than once referred to his disguised flanking movement in Operation Desert Storm as an "end run". What similarities have you drawn between sports and military actions? Have you ever used sports analogies to describe military action or vice versa?

Selection 6

1. You're a young person about to graduate from high school/college looking forward to getting out from under your parent's thumb and taking control of your own life. Then you decide to join the military and soon learn you have no control over your destiny, for a few years anyway. How did giving control of your life to others affect you? Was it just part of the decision or something to deal with and finally accept? Were some parts easier to take than others? Was there something you did in rebellion after you got out?

2. If you were married while being in the military who "controlled" the home front. When our age group was young, the man was expected to be in control of his family. The decisions were his, with maybe some input from his wife. The reality is while you are serving there can be a deployment, an unaccompanied tour or a TDY at any time. So the spouse is left to "control" the home front. He/she gets used to doing things their way with their personality in charge, then you come home and act as if you haven't been away. Was swapping "control" or learning to share it a trial for you? How did you handle the adjustment period upon your return? Was there compromise involved?

3. Control also comes into play when people are in a chain of command. What kind of challenges did you have being controlled/led by another, or if you were in charge was it a trial to treat/control each person fairly and equally?

4. Or, write any other type of control.

Selection 7

Many of the prompts that we have had have been contemplative, invoking sadness, bad memories and tragedy. While my military career had its share of grim and somber moments, the dolefulness has been far outweighed by comical and ludicrous episodes. Soldiers have many proficiencies. But they may be most adept at comical banter, antics, buffoonery, and clowning around. I am hoping that today's prompts will bring out some of those escapades.

1. *"Never tell people how to do things. Tell them what to do and they will surprise you with their ingenuity."* -George S. Patton.
Ingenuity can be used for good causes or shenanigans. Illustrate one instance where American ingenuity was on full display.

2. *"The first virtue in a soldier is endurance of fatigue; courage is only the second virtue."* -Napoleon Bonaparte.
Sleep is a valuable commodity for soldiers, one that is often lacking. Frequently it is the result of the soldier's own blunder. The consequences of being tired can be noteworthy, sometimes with hilarious results. Expound on one.

3. *There are no secrets to success. It is the result of preparation, hard work, learning from failure.* -Colin Powell.
We have all experienced failure. But if you can't laugh at your mistakes... Share one such bungle.

4. *"The reason the American Army does so well in wartime, is that war is chaos, and the American Army practices it on a daily basis."* -from a post-war debriefing of a German General.
It is a good thing that some things never change. Though this quote is from the end of WWII, I can testify that the American Army still practices chaos on a daily basis, at least they did up through June of 2016 when I was retired. Describe some chaos you have witnessed, or maybe even initiated.

5. *"A serious problem in planning against American doctrine is that the Americans do not read their manuals, nor do they feel any obligation to follow their doctrine."* -Soviet observation during the Cold War.
Rules and regulations are not much fun. Unless you don't follow them. Or maybe the rules themselves were lunacy. Recount one such instance.

SELECTION 8

The movie industry has produced a large number of prisoner-of-war films, such as "The Great Escape," "Stalag 17," "The McKinsey Break," "Slaughterhouse-5," "Unbreakable," as well as many, many TV series. We absorbed these shows, no doubt each of us quite differently. Very likely, though, we all pretty much spent the movie time thinking, "Now what would I have done here?" Here's your chance. Consider POW situations from these angles:

A. Prompt #1, *What if you were captured?* What are the first three actions you would take on arrival at your enemy's POW area after capture. Assume you are unwounded. #1? #2? #3? Nonmilitary members can freely participate.

B. Prompt #2, *What if you were captured? [FICTION PROMPT]:* Using your ample talents, what would your story be to your debriefing officer on arriving back to your lines after a harrowing three-day breakout and E&E from the enemy camp.

C. Prompt #3, *Do you have a friend or family member who had been a POW?* Can you share some of his/her story?

D. Prompt #4, *If the idea of enemy' capture is abhorrent to you*: By all means, do create an important few paragraphs on something like: "What three features of a prisoner camp would I set up to house our own enemy combatants? What would be my #1 principle to make the circumstance humane? Have you ever daydreamed about a better way to accept prisoners?.

Selection 9

Food is always a daily topic of discussion. Write about one or more ways it impacted your life or service. Was it good, bad, you ate it anyway, you wanted it, again and again, foreign or Mom's home-cooking. What was memorable and why?

Selection 10

Music goes with us everywhere. What songs bring back military service memories. What did you listen to during your time of active duty? Did you use it to reduce boredom while on any type of duty? Does patriotic music stir you, why or why not? As always, go where the prompt leads.

SELECTION 11

1. Have you discovered something powerful: a person, a place or a talisman that you use to focus on when bad or painful memories are trying to control your thoughts?

2. Symbols surround us. An example would be the Golden Arches for McDonalds or a television theme song. These symbols convey meanings of countless things and vivid images in our everyday life. Then the symbol lingers in our minds to keep that object in our vision and helps us connect our feelings to that object or event.

Every country in the world has symbols that give its citizens a sense of national pride. Among those symbols is a flag. What does our flag mean or represent to you and how do you feel when someone disrespects it?

3. Food and travel seem to be synonymous. In your military or other travels is there a food you had that you now miss or restaurant that you would love to revisit. When you were in the military was there an unavailable food that you couldn't wait to have once you returned to the states? Did it taste as good as you thought it would?

4. "Music can change lives. Whether you are having a good or bad day, the power of music can change one's mood." - Jess Bowen, drummer for the rock band, The Summer Set. Is music a tool in your life? If so, what kind?

5. Or answer any one of the questions Lee Brice asks in the chorus of one of his songs.

>What makes you take a stand?
>Want to get up and dance?
>What makes you laugh, you cry?
>Raise your hands to the sky?
>What keeps you up at night?

SELECTION 12

Prompt #1: Scene Meditation

"Writing is like meditation: You sit breathing in silence, only you add one thing—the writing. Instead of letting thoughts and pictures and feelings go by, you hold on to them. You slow them down. You find the words for them. Writing, you shine light-the light of your intelligence-into a scene of the past, into the dark of forgotten things, fearful things. Writing, you change. And you change the world, even the past. You make history. Write things out, and you won't need to carry memories in your body as pain. The paper will carry your stories. We, your readers, will help you carry your stories. See how light paper is? "A scene is an event, an action in continuous time. Write a scene of joy, a scene of sorrow that happened once. Once upon a time ... One morning... One night, it happened that ... Envision the scene, and don't look away. Tell us—the people here with you what you see, and help us to see it. We want to see it. We want to hear you. Use the other senses too. Something happened—a tragedy, a joy. What was the smell and taste of it, the sound and touch of it?"---Maxine Hong Kingston from the *Fifth Book of Peace*

Prompt #2: To Whom It May Concern:

We recently passed the 13th anniversary of the start of the Iraq War. Writer and Veteran Pete McShane used this anniversary to write a letter on behalf of a dying soldier who served in Iraq. Write your own letter (fiction or nonfiction) to mark this date. Write it to anyone you choose: politician, public official, soldier, spouse, self. (McShane's letter was to President Bush, and can be found on Truthdig website.)

SELECTION 13

A. Prompt #1: How pain shapes us. "Living through inner pain is how we lose our arrogance, our selfishness, and our ignorance. It is how we acquire gentleness and a sense of responsibility, maturity, and capacity for leadership." (Jennifer Hecht, "To Live Is an Act of Courage," *The American Scholar.* Autumn 2013) How has inner pain shaped your outlook on life? Have you become more aggressive or passive? How did that inner pain change you?

B. Prompt #2: A sense of place. "Fort Carson was a world unto itself. The post had everything: a military exchange (the PX) that might have been mistaken for a Walmart, a commissary that stocked multiple varieties of spicy Korean ramen noodles and English crumpets as well as the usual American brands, a Starbucks, a bowling alley, a theater, several gyms and pools, daycare centers, a gas station, a post office, a liquor store, three elementary schools, and a middle school. Also, of course, there were offices, shooting ranges, barracks for single soldiers, simulation centers where soldiers took part in elaborate computerized war games, vast parking lots full of Humvees and tanks, and hangars for helicopters and drones." (Rosa Brooks, *How Everything Became War and the Military Became Everything.* 2016) Describe a military post from your experience. In addition to providing material comforts, what sense of community did it provide?

C. Prompt #3: Influence or colonialism? "Chin Peng was the undisputed leader of the Malayan Communist Party. By a strange and curious twist of fate, with many of his top commanders, to say nothing of the rank and file, he had learned the art of jungle guerrilla warfare from, of all people, the British." (Noel Barber, The War of the Running Dogs. 1971)

SELECTION 14

A. Prompt #1, *Duty* as "taking charge": "I relieve you, Sir," showed up twice in the movie *Caine Mutiny* (1954). The first was standard change-of-command talk when Lt. Cmdr. Queeg (Humphry Bogart) assumed command of Navy mine sweeper USS Caine. The more serious second time, upon Lt. Maryk's (Van Johnson) wrenching the Caine's command from Captain Queeg during the chaos of typhoon conditions. Maryk's original Navy oath was to NOT usurp command. The Services taught us all (sort of) to obey such "higher morality," maybe even mutiny, if duty dictated. Write about where you "took charge" especially as a civilian especially even some small duty, but important in some way.

B. Prompt #2, *Duty*, (speaking of "taking an oath"): we find [Sir] Thomas More (Paul Scofield) in the movie *A* M*an for All Seasons* confronting his friend the Duke of Norfolk about keeping their dangerous talk about King Henry VIII confidential:*MORE: And if the King should command you to repeat what I may say? NORFOLK: I should keep my word to you. MORE: Then what has become of your* oath of obedience *to the King?!* Indeed. Now you be Norfolk and write your answer to Sir Thomas, or to a good friend. Remember—you, the Duke, are also a military man who just got handed a hot choice about *duty*

C. Prompt #3, *Duty* as "debt, obligation, burden": recall Colonel Nicholson (Alec Guinness) in *Bridge on the River Kwai* (1957) talking to the prison camp doctor about why he forces his fellow captives to build the Kwai River bridge, "I hope that the people that use this bridge in years to come will remember how it was built and who built it. Not a gang of slaves, but soldiers, British soldiers, Clipton..." Nicholson's dark, mixed sense of duty cost him in the end. No one succeeded in talking the colonel out of finishing the bridge, to the harm of all else. When have you had to be "the best *man* in the room" and use your learned idea of *duty* to change other people's actions, probably to your personal cost?

D. Prompt #4: You have no duty to respond or react to any of these prompts. Write whatever you think will add to the success of our session today, about *duty* or anything else. This will certainly be anything you can create.

Selection 15

Prompt #1 To go unarmed into battle is an extraordinary thing. Military Chaplains have chosen to serve not only their God, but the men and women who must fight these wars. They see the worst examples of combat and still rally to inspire and comfort soldiers at their most vulnerable moments. Thousands of Chaplains have served our military throughout its history. Eight of these Chaplains received the Medal of Honor. Most recently, Father Emil Kapaun (Catholic) was honored (posthumously) by President Obama for his actions as a Prisoner of War in Korea in 1951. Write a story of a Military Chaplain (or a religious leader) that inspired you in some way.

Prompt #2 Among the most memorable military stories we have involve "how bad we had it"' during Basic Training. "Mom, these sergeants are just so unfair. They pick on me for no reason and call me names!" "You should have seen the chow line. It was so long and we only got 5 minutes to eat our food!" "I just can't remember everything...Left, right, left, Present Arms, and About Face...I can't do anything right!" Just some of the many examples of the "scariest" time in our lives. But was it that scary? Did you see the big picture? Did you just want to go home?Write a story that brings to life some of the trials you faced as a young soldier.

Prompt #3 "The nation needs men (and women) who think in terms of service to their country and not in terms of their country's debt to them." - Omar N. BradleyWhen General Bradley uttered these words, I wonder if he was struggling with the mood of the country, or perhaps with his own understanding of societal trends.Write an essay that unpacks this statement for the modern era (2018).

SELECTION 16

Throughout our American history, each generation of warriors has their own style of music that has ranged from inspiration and power, to revenge and depression, and every emotion in between. Is there a genre, group or song that you held close during your time of service? A few examples are Big Band, Dixieland, Patriotic songs, British Invasion, Rock, Country, Reggae, contemporary, jazz and countless others. Is there a single song that brings you back there? Several songs? Please explore the theme of music and tell us why it has a certain significance to you.

The Holiday season is upon us once again. Do you have a feeling about the Holidays? Do they make you happy, sad, or somewhere in between? Tell us a story of a deployment during a Holiday or what goes through your mind as you celebrate your religion and spirituality or curse the swarms of people crowding the streets and stores to buy things for themselves or others.

Selection 17

1. "Attention getting. As Americans we have an expectation of cordiality toward each other. We know this is the proper way to interact. War is not cordial. War is basic. From the first day of Basic Training we learn a language that in civilian life is seen as unacceptable (examples: WTF, AOR, Point, Article 15, *didi mau, frag, hump*, - well, you get the picture). Write a story from your experiences (more than one if you like) that demonstrate the need for basic behavior to survive the crude nature of war and combat, and how your adoption of basic communication might have helped you."

2. Military v. Home front mindset – Returning from Reserve Drill, a Field Training Exercise, or even a Combat deployment, our mindset changes. This can be positive or negative, but seldom neutral. Describe for us a change of mindset that may have been altered by your military experience(s). Example: I always leave at least one car length in front of me in case there is an emergency and I have to get away quickly."

3. The 15:17 to Paris is a Clint Eastwood film coming to theaters on 9 FEB 2018. It depicts three Americans who discover a terrorist plot aboard a train and how they responded. Most people avoid the struggle or the risk that makes something worth doing. Describe an instance when you encountered such a struggle and took a risk.

4. Images of war do not have to be those of direct combat. The crying child holding her baby sister while fleeing something evil. Perhaps a person bathing in a cesspool of filth because it's the only water for miles. Children, the infirm, or the elderly being transported in crude wheelbarrows because they are no longer welcome in their homeland. Describe a scene you have witnessed that still plagues your mind to this day.

5. Something Funny? A character? Maybe an instance when you got away with something?

6. Write whatever you want.

Made in the USA
Coppell, TX
09 December 2020